There's More to Life than Death

There's More to Life than Death

Anne Forrest

Bridge House

British Library Cataloguing in Publication Data
A Record of this Publication is available from the British
Library

ISBN 978-1-914199-72-1

This edition published 2024 by Bridge House Publishing
Manchester, England

Cover painting © Terry Mart

For my grandson, William Andrew Parker, and George Stanley Parker

Contents

Introduction

I'm pleased to present my first collection of short-stories.

All the tales live in the 20th Century, so nostalgia and textuality may catch the reader by the throat and take them back to the portal of another time.

In exploring these tales, the reader will encounter an uncanny view of happenings beyond and behind the comfortable, and where my imagination has inveigled its way onto the page.

My eclectic taste in reading and writing comes from my childhood love of Enid Blyton (cosy atmosphere by the bucket load) and later, Cormac McCarthy where his beautifully written prose transcends the darkest of happenings. The writings of McCarthy inspire me hugely giving me the confidence to write some stories without speech-marks. Included in this collection of tales, 'Quinn', 'The Molly Boys' and 'Warm Flannelette' are such attempts; they are taken from my unpublished picaresque novel *Quinn*.

There are many descriptions of the word 'uncanny'; let us settle for 'disquieting'.

This book is a work of fiction. Any resemblance to settings or persons living or dead is purely inevitable.

Quinn

Nothing is clearer to this man than he must keep going, moving on so that nothing catches up with him and his sin.

He trudged through the medieval town of Conwy, a numbing coldness creeping up through his thin boots and into his bones, he exited by the upper gate, and at Town Ditch he left the ancient walls behind and walked upwards. At his back the Castle, Telford's suspension bridge, the Smallest House on the harbour; boats, fishermen, trawlers and mussel-men who sometimes found pearls: and the population known by their birthright, as Jackdaws.

The last of the pale winter sun was starting to set and the evening frost was quick on its heels; he tightened his jacket collar and prised a fat safety pin off a card of six, standing with his rucksack wedged between his knees trying to work fast against the cold. He went on towards the bluey hills, passed through a hamlet of twelve or so homesteads and on to a good track towards the small village of Rowen. Two miles beyond that and he reached the steep lane, grass-cobbled and inhospitable, and between tall dry-stone walls up he trekked until he came to an iron barred gate tethered to its stone pillar with curls of wire. His hand burnt and stuck fast to the bar as he heaved; he shoved it into his mouth and cursed, tasting frost iron and welts rising. He closed the gate with his foot and shoulder; a derelict cottage stood melancholy and black against the sky-lit land, it floated in a lake of minute stars as Jack o' Lantern twinkled above ground like some fantastic fairyland blooming, and the utter beauty of it was not lost on him. He turned again and moon-blanched hills lay ahead and to his right and to his left. Something red-warm in that cold white slunk away finding a shadow and then disappeared into it. As if he were at one with the place and of its core he stayed taking in the quiet and melting into it. He bent his head and lifted up his frozen foot to walk on.

Up and up colder as he went. Dirty looking sheep huddled in their pens chewing and staring and as if wondering about this man thinly dressed. Two more miles and he wanted further.

The man had seen over thirty-five winters, none colder he felt, and he'd faced more than five of these with neither kith nor kin. Over on his left he saw a small church nestling like a squatting frog in the dip, its glistening roof floating in a grey-white shroud of icy hillside mist. He fancied he heard the bell toll and stopped to listen. Head inclined toward the motionless bell he appeared to be intent on what he heard. He found he could not stop walking, the moon filling the sky with its hugeness and painting the land clear and the path ahead white as with salt. Mountain ponies still and watchful as he strode. A muffled shr-shrump, a stamp, a whistle of mane being shaken in the night. He went on. Two more miles and the night as light as day when he came upon a tiny house set in a poor looking place, a lamp shining in an upstairs window. Black trees, tall and dwarfing it. He circled the place and saw little sign of life. He made for the far outhouse with bales of hay stacked in blocks and slept and dreamt of a screaming banshee who wrapped him in her arms and would not let go of him. Then she did and he drifted off again. A monstrous pink-footed rodent dragged its swollen hindquarters across the floor; already warfarined with its belly in liquid knots, the rat moved without purpose along the littered flags. A soft and whispering warmth blew evenly and sourly, the rat turned from the man's breath and in its own helpless wretchedness, poured fluidly away into the darkness. The man fended off the banshee with a small sound and a wave of his hand; shifting himself he made little alteration to his bedding so slender was he. In a mantle of feed sacking, his face, etched noble and easy in repose, rested on hands fast as if in prayer. He slept on. In the night that was light as day a fox barked and his

11

vixen came to him. Not long afterwards the rooks started to claim their territory, cawing, croncking and making a lazy disturbance above the trees in the icy dawn.

Now he must be in a Turkish palace, an exotic house of wealth, of brightness, picking out jewels of the richest colours, shafts cutting through ruby red and amber and emerald green, through facets of diamonds glinting and shimmering and sliding slowly down the frosted window-pane to gather in a rainbow stream. Mote ridden light beamed earthward and touched jars of captured summer: of seed riddled raspberry, redcurrant, blackcurrant, of luscious Victoria plum and Denbigh plum, goosegogs and quince; the light played on Kilners of ginger chutney, pickled cabbage magenta and purple, and on the detached eyes of pickled onions, all these stood in row upon glorious row next to raised sacks of potatoes and turnip and swede for winter plateful's of steaming buttered *stwnch rwdan*. He opened his eyes fully, salivating and wiping his mouth with the back of his hand, and sat up. He made himself decent, ready to set out into the early morning frost. Knotholes in the old wood told him that it was no warmer today. Before he left he opened a jar of pickled eggs and ate two then ate two more and packed away some potatoes to bake the next time he had a fire. He placed some coppers on top of the jar and walked into the yard to consider his next move. Suddenly a light showed up a red and white curtain at the kitchen window. He must knock and make himself known.

A woman of about forty cracked open the door, peering at him and over his shoulder as if to find answers there. What do you want? Anxious and twisting a cloth into a teacup. What do you want this hour of the day?

I... I just knocked to thank you. For my bed. Y'see I slept in your outhouse last night and was grateful to get out of the temperature indeed I was.

12

Last night.

Yes. Yes I did.

You been here before?

No. First time up here.

Not a few months ago. A year?

No. No. Look I've bothered you and I'm sorry, so I am. Can I do anything in return? I'd be pleased really. Feel much better about things.

She said, looking bewildered, No, you're welcome.

Nothing moved, not her eyes, nor her hands, and her breathing seemed suspended. An icy gust whirled and shifted crisp leaves in the porch; weightless they danced and lilted and settled. Then: I need to go, and she made to close the door on him. A sound stopped her. Her face contorted, I... He saw her clutch her cardigan and hug it to her throat strangling the words. Beneath the cardigan she wore a once bright wrap-around pinafore over a frock of grey flannelette, her hair in pins. Bare legs and bedroom slippers with cream fur pom-poms.

Yes, I should be off too. But he didn't move. Keep out the cold now. Looks like it might snow.

Oh, no, she murmured.

Looks like it. You're sure I can't stack wood. Chop it.

No.

He turned to leave.

A screech rang out from inside, upstairs. Maa-a-aam!

I have to go. O God help us! And then all hell broke out into the tableaux: Come in'n please try to help... and she stumbled ahead of him.

The child was only about fifteen. She'd used the last of her strength to call. Her head lay back as if twisted and she already appeared dead so blue-white was her face, and wet. A girl baby was stuck fast between her bloodied legs, a marbled bottom and one leg out.

It's here, O God, she having it and it's breached! I thought it would never come… Two days she's been at it one way or the other and *O, Iesu Grist* I can't get it out! Tugging and pulling this slimy thing to no avail and, Help me girl, push, pu-ush for Christ's sake. But the girl could not oblige.

For all his years he knew nothing of childbirth but knew he could not allow the woman to know it. See to the girl, he said evenly, Keep her alive. A drink, water or something. I'll see to… With infinite gentleness he eased his fingers into her and as if his touch triggered it, she involuntarily shuddered as if it had nothing to do with her, and shoved and spewed out something that would not have gone amiss in a freak show at a country fair. Having made a noise of sorts it was lying in the mess, motionless save for a tiny clawing of her right hand that was joined firmly to her elbow. It was difficult to look at, to see this mistake. To see an eye where a nose should be and no mouth to speak of. Dear Lord.

Check on her, he said jutting his chin in the new mother's direction, shock rendering him quiet spoken. See *she's* all right at least.

The woman's horrified stare. She backed away.

A knife. A knife too, for God's sake get a blade of some sort.

Now he saw the blood. Try to stem that flow, he said more urgently. Cloths and things, towels. You have plenty?

I'll get them. But she did not move.

Move, he said into her face. Quickly.

He sliced through the cord and left it and covered up the girl's legs. There was a wooden box, an orange box and in it a blanket and sheets cut to size. He carefully enveloped the baby's tiny body, folding and tightening the sheet until only the head showed, hair a bloody honey colour. A blind and no doubt deaf infant; he was surprised to see the lips, misshapen and fish-like trying to make suckling motions. He watched it. This precious God-given life attempting to take what it knew was hers. By the time the woman came to look at her granddaughter, the child was dead and the Lord had not had a say in it.

You'd better concentrate on your daughter…

She'll be all right, now? A whisper.

I think you need a doctor for her.

No! God, No.

You must. She's draining away. I can go back into the town with a truck…

She put a hand out. No. She'll be all right…

Well into the next night the girl lay still as death, only her hoarse breathing and florid rings on her cheeks like half-crowns, showed she was alive. He and the woman tended her and he tended the woman with hot tea and soft words. She'll be all right. She's young. And healthy; she was healthy, wasn't she? And the woman nodding and nodding and saying little of any sense.

He spoke carefully again. What about the doctor? Just to check her. You can't lose her as well.

She didn't answer him but shook her head firmly and slowly and pursed her mouth. He had no right to interfere further.

If you're certain.

I am certain. Certain of that. Anyway, she's improving, look. The girl's face had not altered and her breathing was no easier. Look. She's better I tell you! A sob from the woman holding her throat as if to strangle herself.

All right… But *you* must keep strong then. For her. Sleep, if you can.

I couldn't.

You might.

No. I'll be all right.

You've had no rest. None for days by the look of things.

15

I can manage.

Early dusk fell and gauze-like lavender settled on the room downstairs. By now, the woman in her chair and studying the fire.

You sleep now, she said to him. You've done enough for us. Her chin lowered into her knuckled hand and she listening to the gas pop and splutter from the coal.

I still have something to do.

She looked at him tilting her face.

I'll see to it just now.

What?

You have a spade... in one of the sheds? He stood, his arms loose by his sides.

Back to the coals. Dear Lord! Yes, softly.

I'll manage... He stood a while looking with her into the fire, then made to go outside. I'll find things.

The woman spoke as if to the flames in the grate. Seren, she said. She has to have a name. Seren. It means Star.

Yes.

The man carried the bundle now shrouded in the sheet and newspaper, a spade over his shoulder slipping and sliding over the yard on crystal sheets of ice to stumble and rearrange the bundle under his arm, and open a side gate, quietly though there was no one to hear it creak, no one to see him, head down going along the narrow pathway brushing aside frost covered fantasies of hedgerow, to hear the crunch underfoot and the owl hoot inquiringly. A clear sky again. He came out into a white field, clumps of grass forming fairyland castles, the heap of dung a strange white-capped hill. He tapped the spade on the hill and even the dung had frosted hard. He walked round inspecting every place and found an old hen house staved in and shoved half under the hedge. The wire netting cage now home to feral cats that wailed and spat at him as he kicked the coop over and tested the ground. He cursed for not having a fork. He removed the paper carefully, wadded it and slipped it into his pocket, and laid the baby bundle in the winter wonderland, stiff now and watched over by yellow slits huddled beneath the hedge, the cats making strange growling noises and baring their teeth and yowling through them. He struck the ground that had been kept from freezing by the warm pulse of a wild animal. He dug through the acrid stench of cat pee until he reached an appropriate depth and hoped that the soft and pliable bones would not stay too long and that they would melt and nourish the spring celandine and the wood sorrel. And that her being would have some purpose. Before he picked up the swaddled baby now glistening with frozen dew specks, he shook out a cloth he'd had a mind to bring, placed it over the face now quite beautiful in his eyes, and cushioned it behind the head and stood with it a while. He bent and lowered her gently into the earth, her cold cradle now powdered and silvery. He looked up at the vastness and marvelled at the perfect placing of each star. He mouthed *Pater Nostra qui es in coelis... Our Father who art in heaven...* Could he ever be forgiven?

Almost twenty-four hours since he'd first knocked, he tapped on the back door again and eased himself in quietly, wiping snowflakes off his sleeves. It was as if this was that first time. The woman, standing there, cloth and teacup.

It did snow then?

A flurry. It won't last. Too cold I think.

I'm just making a pot.

The dawn was just unlocking the room and cast a cold light over it. I'll stoke the fire, he said.

There's paper-sticks, cinders, it'll catch again.

He knelt down and took the poker and levelled the dying embers. He took three plaited sticks and arranged them then he fetched from his pocket the wadded

17

newspaper and placed that on top. Large cinder shells on top of that. A handful of black nubs. We'll soon get the place warmed up. How is the girl… your daughter?

Sleeping. A good sleep now it seems. She waved the cup limply. Have you… Where have…?

Somewhere quiet. Out of the way of things…

She nodded. Best.

I said something, you know, when I laid her in.

She nodded again and brought up her face to find his eyes. He did not let her find them.

They drank the tea. She sliced and buttered bread and spread it with honey, passed it to him and took up her place in the fireside chair. He finished eating.

You rest now, she said.

I think I will. You're all right?

I will be. Will you be warm enough with the straw? Take a blanket. Anything you want. A quilt. There's only her and me. She did not move from her chair.

Thank you. May I take more bread?

Anything. She sat still, her arms invisible in a shawl. An age-old posture. Her hair now loosed from their pins fell in slender caramel coloured fingers about her face and on the nape of her neck. Her hopelessness touched Quinn and he wanted to reach out and gently push the hair from her face and stroke that neck until she might weep against him.

There's just the two of you, here, looking after this?

Yes, since eighteen months now. I'm widowed.

I'm sorry.

She looked as if that sorrow was a long way away, as if it had been overtaken.

Will you need help? Just till she's stronger?

I will. I will, dear God. I don't know what we're going to do.

I can stay. For a while.

18

Yes. Yes, please.

He stood with an eiderdown draped over his arm. Will you go up and rest too?

Yes, I'd best be near her. 'Case she calls... And you can wash in the back scullery whenever you need. Anything you want, take it. She waved him gone, wearily.

Thank you, Mrs...

Mostyn. Alys Mostyn.

I'm known as Quinn, Mrs Mostyn. Shout out if you need me.

The following days weather mirrored the silent house. The sky plain and dull holding back the snow. The frost lost its prettiness and little moved about the place: yard cats, the dog, hens, all lethargic. The dunnocks' *'tseep'* less shrill; the *'pink, pink,'* of the chaffinch quieter. The shriek of the barn owl less piercing. As if all the small life in that bleak place knew of the sadness there; as if they too, knew of the hurt. A wind chime fashioned from all kinds of childish things hung motionless from the limb of a stunted fruit tree, itself bent the way of many winter winds: tin-foil bells made from milk bottle tops, broken crockery and glass, green, blue, tied and fastened with little pieces of plaited string; midnight blue mussel shells and creamy pink cockle shells threaded with cotton. Silent now to match the mood. An enamel pan, shallow and half sunk into the earth, a bucket half full of feed swollen and grotesque. Dereliction had come rapidly to this farmstead.

Christmas 1959 came quietly and uncelebrated; none of the three people in that place wanted to dwell upon the birth of a baby, Christ-child or not. New Year's Eve saw little difference from any of those awful days. Alys twiddled the knobs on the wireless: A bit of music might help raise our spirits for a while, she said sighing. They sat with glasses of port and some beers. The child who'd had to grow up so violently sat reading the *Girl*; she nibbled at cheese straws

19

she'd learned to make at school, and sipped lemonade. In between the wailing bagpipes, riotous stamping and singing from somewhere in Scotland, and humour from Wee Winnie and Wee Jock McCree, one of Harold Macmillan's government ministers kept interrupting with talk of the new decade about to hit Britain: *After the dark days and aftermath of war, we are catching up with and overtaking those dark days.* He shouted as if he were in direct competition with the Hogmanay Night revellers: *Nineteen-Sixty will herald a new era! An era the likes of which has never been anticipated before in the history of our Country...* Wee Winnie told a joke in a thick accent, which rendered it unintelligible; she and Wee Jock screamed with raucous laughter and the sound of a huge drum banged and the band played a lively reel – a strange muffled sound with a background crackling as the waves travelled the air and somehow found this little farmstead. Again, the minister: *We will instigate policies of peace, liberty and law; we will capitalise on the noble National Health Service, the Education Act and expand the roads and highways programme. We will raise living standards and encourage the enjoyment of more leisure time – even as I speak, one in three families today has a car or motor-cycle, two out of three is able to rent a television set, and twice as many are now taking holidays away from home...* The band's noise grew into fervour and the Scots Master of Ceremonies marked time: One Hour to Go, he announced above the din, One hour before we say Giud-by Tae the Fifties... One hour before we welcome in 1960! Alys Mostyn turned the knob low and said: It's time I went to bed.

Quinn said he'd turn in too. The mother helped her daughter up off the chair: the child still could not move well: You too my girl, she said wearily. Tomorrow's another day.

Perfect

Consciousness came to him slowly as if it were holding back a conspiracy. Poverty of sound yielded a low hoot then a sharp kee-wick as Tawny Owl cut leisurely through the night air, her flight fast and silent. Quarry cave-bats crisscrossed above the man's half-slit eyes like tiny mute souls. Over the oak and ash, the moon came up for a minute and iced the trees a salty white. When it disappeared, he saw the constellation as if it were written in a witch's hand, all gold and silvery against the midnight blue and giving a facetious message. When he moved, the warm, damp patch turned cold and he did not find any more comfort. On one elbow, he shook his head slowly where stones rattled within and left an uneasy echo and a bilious sickness. He heard the slice of a spade, smelled newly shifted soil and wafting honeysuckle on this summer night. The owl called hooo, a tremulous sound. Something told him to make no noise, and to lie as if not of this world.

Eventually came the dawn. Birdcalls shrill and sweet and clear, and with the gentle heat, orange capped toadstools and scalloped shelves of fungi. Morning dew glistened pearl-like on slender fingers of leaf. From the rich carpet, the pleasant scent of Herb Robert. Still lying cramped, the man was wedged up against a bedstead-stop in the crumbling stone wall. He hadn't meant to fall here. He swivelled his head, alert, the hangover gone. Until the next time. All overgrown with funnels of blue and white convolvulus, the rusty bedhead looked as pretty as a decorated tree hung with pale china bells.

Two men tramped by. Quarry workers. Even though a truck would take them to the top without effort they tramped the woods talking quietly saying little of importance. He saw them, they looked easy, so at one with the place as if at the blink of his eye, they might blend into the luscious copse.

Dad worked up there y'know.

Duw, hello Jackdaw. Didn't y'make it home last night?

I was with him.

Aye.

When the blast went off.

Aye. Yes.

Killed him stone dead. Mam said.

Aye, dad told me all about it, Jackdaw. He was there himself, remember?

I was only four.

Aye. Yes, I remember like it was yesterday, boy. Dad came home and told us. Bad day that.

Day not to be forgot, eh? Jackdaw's cackle-cough echoed and shut up the birds. On earlies?

Aye. Yes. Yes, indeed.

You on all week?

All week, Jackdaw.

How's it going up there?

Nothing changes y'know, boy.

See you later, then.

Nothing surer, they said, and walked on.

Dad came last night y'know; I heard him. Jackdaw nudged his head into his topcoat collar so that his voice did not carry and touch the men.

Jack Lavender Lewis once had a full family. Mother Alice May Lewis, father Joshie Lewis and two brothers who lived only long enough to be named. Edward and Thomas; Jackdaw, being the only survivor of the triplets.

For almost fifty years, Jackdaw's dad lay in pieces above his infant sons in the old cemetery a mile away. They say that his head was never found, and they couldn't be sure what other parts were missing. They went on to say what a

22

good job it was that young Jackdaw had wandered off to gather weed-flowers for his mam while Joshie was fixing a gate for a bit of overtime, and just got the tail-end of the blast and that no-one got the blame for it, and that if it happened today there'd be loads of compensation and that Jackdaw could live in a castle or somewhere nice.

Who needs a castle? Jackdaw was as happy as a robin at Christmas in his sett-man's dug-out. Dark as a ditch until his eye adjusted then creamy light with granite dust. His mother was still alive in Fechan Hospital, but her memory was dead. She'd been put there in 1959 when it was a mad-house and stayed there when it got its new name. It had a view of the river in all its moods. *Perffaidd.* Jackdaw said when anyone asked after her. Perfect. With a view like that.

How's y'mam, Jackdaw? Someone would ask.

So-so, y'know.

Seen her lately.

Not quite.

She's OK though?

Fine. Lovely view on it. *Perffaidd. Perffaidd i Mam.* Perfect for Mam.

Once, Jackdaw had a nain and a taid and three aunties and two uncles and a kind of cousin who didn't really belong in blood. He still had one aunt. Auntie Mori lived in Upper Hill street as near to the woods as dammit. *Perffaidd i Jacdaw.* Perfect. Auntie Mori saw to him. Saw that he had clothes and bathroom facilities. Saw that he had bread and milk and cheese and apples from the little tree next to the house and eggs from the hens in the patch of garden. Auntie Mori saw to his benefits and led the Social to think he lived at number thirty-five. She always kept a bed made.

He could hear her now talking to the chickens and telling them how well they laid and how nice and brown the shells were. He saw the small round shape of her richly flowered pinny as his aunt perched atop the home-made ladder style. On tiptoe she leaned over and lowered the bag, her tightly bound bosom straining and her breath puffing and panting.

Welsh sing-song in the quiet. Jackdaw she called. Jackdaww.

He carted the bag up to his hut and found she had put in two new pencils and a small hand-sewn book of smooth paper sheets. He munched on a breakfast of crisp bacon and fried egg sandwiches smothered in brown sauce he kept in a box and washed it all down with spring-water tea. Then he slept.

At noon he heard the men's boots crunching soft and heavy on the worn path and he could hear the music of pan lids; the smell of a stew cooking. He didn't have to look out to know the men would sprint one after the other, each over his own back wall and some to take a short cut. And he'd hear them again going back up, and again when they came home at the end of the day and then to find that there had been a breakdown and more men would have to go up and fix the crusher before the Sunday shift.

Hiya!

Hello there, Jackdaw. *S'mae.* How's y'mam?

So-so y'know. Need any help up there?

Might do. Coming up with us?

In a flash, Jackdaw stuffed his pencil stubs into a string-drawn bag and put it and his book into a top pocket and walked with the men. A carbon copy, boots falling in step.

It was one-thirty in the morning when they left each other to jump in a reverent quiet over the wall whispering, Ta-ra now. Cheerio. *Nos da.*

Jackdaw tired out with the sheer responsibility of overseeing the men's work, said Ta-ra.

Nos Da, Jackdaw. Diolch am dy help.

24

We did OK didn't we lads? As per!

Fine. We did a fine job, boy.

For a long time, Jackdaw sat and took in the night. Its perfection surrounded him as he shared the sounds of quiet. He lit a cigarette, the pinprick glow moved slowly and brightened at each puff. He lay against his warm doorframe and breathed in the scent of the sleeping wood. *Perffaidd.*

Monday morning. The warning hooter howled. Jackdaw put his fingers in his ears as the blasting began. Long and rumbling. Sometimes he could feel the draught of that day fifty years ago when his head felt light as a feather. Sometimes he heard the loud silence which occurred afterwards. Always he remembered the sleepiness and the voices as they came nearer. Calling out, Jackdaw, Jackdaw *bach*. Always he tried not to see his mam's face framed in hospital white and green, when she said over him, *Lle ma dy dad, fy mab fach.* Where is your dad, my little boy?

And then the all clear.

He shook his head to bring himself back to today, and the sound of boys calling to him.

Whee-whoo. Whee-whoo.

Hiya lads, he answered.

Watcha Jackdaw. Got any cigs?

Plenty.

Any booze?

Watch it! No school?

Teachers rest.

The boys rummaged among Jackdaw's things. Squashed cigarettes.

Christ, Jackdaw, what the fuck've you been doing with these.

Language, Georgie Fellows!

25

Yeah, yeah.

Hey Tubs, I told you no booze.

What's this then.

Mine.

Tight-arse.

Put it back. Sit down.

Boys and man-boy settled back against the motley seating.

Put that bottle down, Tubs. And leave them pictures alone.

But they're good Jackdaw. Bloody good. Get these lads…

Leave them.

For fuck's sake Tubs, leave the fucking pictures.

Language Georgie. There's no need. I've told you before.

Okay, Okay.

In the tiny sound-proof earth-room, trillions of motes danced in the shaft of warm sunlight from the post-card windowpane, waltzing, turning, spinning. Quickly shrouded in swirls of smoke, Pebo Watson blew rings which disappeared among the crucified garments hung along the prop shafts: a navy donkey jacket and scarf filmed in grey-white dust. A pair of black pants clipped by the waist to a hanger claiming *J.O. Owen Outfitters* in dull gold script. White-grey shirts and a black tie for funerals. Jeans.

The knocking came among shouts of, Jackdaw Lewis open up! Come on now!

Christ! What the fuck…

Two policemen stood against the blinding light like something from a Sunday school picture.

Not so fast you lot.

We haven't done nothing.

No?

No.

Nevertheless.

What's up, Alun?

Just a few questions Jackdaw. This is sergeant Collier.

New?

Newish.

Oh. What's up. No harm here y'know.

I know that Jackdaw. Just a few questions eh. Out y'come lads and stand right here. The officer nodded the sergeant into the hut with his chin. Just a quick speck eh, Jackdaw.

Fine by me.

Names and addresses from you lot.

You know who we are.

Aye. Well… well get home straight away and someone'll call to have a talk later.

We haven't done nothing. Honest.

I know that lads. Just get home eh? Stick to the path. Your mams'll be waiting.

Three pairs of legs ran like the wind, soles flashing in the grass and kicking up stones and bits.

The sergeant came out shaking his head.

Alun Milton whose dad had shared a school desk with Jackdaw on the odd occasion he went, nodded.

Jackdaw said, Come on Alun. What the hell's up?

Not a lot for you to worry about, Jackdaw. What time did you get home night before last?

Night before last?

Yes. Saturday night.

Saturday. Night.

What time did you get home?

Didn't get home.

What?

Didn't get home. Fell by the wayside. His nervous eyes darted, and he laughed at his own humour.

Amy at the Quarryman's said you were in.

'Sright.

What time did you leave?

Haven't got a watch.

Was it late on?

Yes.

Last to leave?

Nearly.

About eleven fifteen? Quarter past eleven?

About that.

Did you see anyone there not local?

Yeh. Blond fella. Small. Sat with Tracy.

Tracy James?

Yeh.

Alun Milton glanced at Collier, and asked Jackdaw.

What time did they leave?

Leave?

Yes. What time did they leave the pub.

Before me.

Jackdaw?

Aa-bout an hour before me.

An hour.

Yes.

You sure?

About.

What about, *about* ten thirty. Half past ten.

Aye. That's about it.

You ever see the blond chap before?

No. A stranger. English he was, I could tell.

OK. Fair enough Jackdaw. That's what others say too. Now, Tracy didn't get home after her night out with the blond fellow. Not been seen since then.

Run off d'you mean?

Maybe. But her mam said she wouldn't do that. Never.

28

'Sright. Not Tracy.

Know Tracy, do you? The sergeant asked.

O'course I do. I know her mam. Everybody knows Tracy. His eyes sought Alun Milton's for confirmation.

Yes. That's right. What did you do yesterday Jackdaw?

Went up with the men, then... just drawing and things, Alun. You know me.

Stayed here did you, in the woods?

As per. Then went to Auntie Mori's. Sunday dinner y'know.

The afternoon was perfect. *P'nawn perffaidd.* He could hear the kids calling in the distance. Laughing. Playing tip, on the piece of ground outside Crimea Bank, right in front of their houses. Playing hide and seek. And the silence they made when the finder was searching among the bushes was loud as a drum. The birds were lazily quiet. Twittering, cheeping, gossiping among themselves.

Jackdaw perched on a square oil-tin and sliding off it as he worked. Shit! Useless. And he pitched it as far as he could into Teifion's work yard from where it had come. He heard the clash and clang and old Tei's foul mouth. Bass-tad Jack-dor.

He nestled down, legs folded underneath him. Bending and peering and melting into the woods he loved. Finding treasures to mirror in his sketchbook. He could draw good Auntie Mori said. You should see his pictures if he'd let you. But he won't.

Jackdaw didn't know he could draw well. Jackdaw if he thought about it at all, thought everyone had his precision. Took it for granted that everyone walked about with a box of watercolour paints in their jacket pocket. Thought everyone sharpened and shaped pencils. He thought everyone used up best part of the day seeking out parties of toadstools and clusters of hazel nuts and branches of acorns in their knobbly cups, and collecting bunches of leaves and ferns and wildflowers to put in a glass jam-jar or stoneware pot. Mostly he sketched in perspective making neat colour notes in the margin, and sometimes his pencil took on a life of its own riding the page as if it had wings and a solitary eye. Jackdaw didn't know it, but he was a fine, botanical artist.

He was near the bedstead hung with pale china-bells and was creating a latticework of twisting stems around the dull brass rails. There was no wrinkling of Jackdaw's simple brow, no pursing of his childish lips. Easily his eyes penetrated the lush growth and took in the rich green icicles of moss, the white shy-flowered wood sorrel. The common dog violet with its mauve-purple petals and rosettes of leaves. His pencil followed the lines of a miniature fern which uncurled through the eye-socket of a half-exposed bone-yellow skull. As Jackdaw's eyes adjusted to this unexpected host, his nostrils again smelled the shifted earth of Saturday night.

Three hours later in the cordoned off wood, two mysteries had been solved. Tracy James lay unearthed now, her pink jumper dragged up around her armpits, her short brown suede skirt about her waist; and about her neck, an obscene blue-red welt.

She was now bagged in black and would be carried gently down the slope towards the path.

Having traversed the woodland as the foxes' plaything for half a century, the missing head of Jackdaw's dad, disturbed by the blond fella's digging, looked rested in its plastic caul.

First published in *Cautiously Tiptoeing... Out of the Light* Sept 2020

Spelling the Words

In the background the television screen was filled with a cream dress, yards and yards of flounce-y cream and a smiling Lady Diana Spencer waving and waving and the crowds cheering madly. Trumpets and music filled the room again as Prince Charles was shown for the umpteenth time marrying his princess. Taking a break from watching the TV, and in-between her running out to the street party, Chrissy frowned in concentration as she placed the ivory-coloured tiles on the board: P.I.S.S., she spelled and swirled the tiles over the table and chose more letters, added another S and hissed *Pisssss* into her hand. More letters and spelled SHIT. and FUCK.

Well done, Chrissy, I think this is helping, don't you? Dr Moffat's idea is really working.

Chrissy's head clicked from side to side and she made a *ch-ck, ch-ck* sound. But I still want to say it, she said. I still want to *say* the words. *Click-click. Ch-ck, ch-ck.*

But you didn't, darling; we won't count that little whisper. Then her mother put more letters ion the board – WELL DONE CHRISSY KEPPLE.

BUGGER, replied Chrissy. BALLS.

With a wry smile, Miriam Kepple thought, Well, her spelling's tip-top anyway! She sighed and suggested that the Scrabble board be moved away until later (close at hand of course, so that it could be easily reached).

Right, out you go, the cakes are on the kitchen table and don't forget the drinks, her mother said. I'm sure the kids are ready for more, oh, and take that last bit of bunting…

As Chrissy made for the kitchen, Miriam heard her say under her breath: Bloody, bloody-bitch, bugger-bastard. Ignoring her, Miriam sighed again. What a mystery. What a bloody mystery, and she smiled and thought, it's catching! Her young daughter was using words never heard in the house; no-one knew where they came from and why she kept uttering them. It didn't make sense, none of it did. The psychiatrist's idea of getting her to spell the words instead of saying them was a good one, she had to admit, but she wished they could find out what had turned their sweet, eleven-year-old child into this foul-mouthed girl. But playing Scrabble was lovely, Ken, Chrissy and she around the table, often tiles face-up and each of them choosing letters to spell out messages: YOU ARE DOING BETTER WE LOVE YOU CHRISSY. Chrissy took the opportunity to express herself in her new, filthy language: FUCK, she might spell back. Sometimes they played properly with tiles face-down, each taking seven and making up words; they allowed Chrissy to use the dictionary – no wonder her vocabulary and spelling was exceptional. School said that. Among all the negative reports, the teachers all said that...

Hurry up with those cakes, darling, and don't snap your head back so sharply, you'll hurt yourself.

Ch-ck.

Ken arrived home about 7pm. After filling his wife in on his day's activities at work, he said, Are you worried about tomorrow?

Of course, I am, aren't you? I still can't make out why Dr Moffat wants to see us so urgently. I don't know what we'll do if he says she must go away to that special school. I know she's getting worse and not fit to be with other children in the class or in any public place for that matter, but to that residential place... how will we tell her?

It was the one thing they feared, that awful sounding Home with talk of 'electric shock' treatments. But if no-one knew what the problem was after nearly two years of doctors, clinics, hospitals and two different psychiatrists, what was the alternative? She couldn't go on like this for ever. Miriam and Ken didn't have a good night, and as soon as Chrissy was settled with her gran, her parents left for the hospital and Chrissy watched the Royal Wedding scenes again.

It was lunchtime when Miriam and Ken arrived home. Gran made cups of tea. Miriam got out the Scrabble board: Come and sit down, Chrissy, we've got something to tell you, love.

The child looked terrified. Trembling and shaking and throwing her head back she said, I know what it is, you've tried to tell me before. Warned me. I'm mad and bad, aren't I? No-one I know clicks and ticks like me, no-one says those awful words... Dr Moffat said they don't know what's wrong with me and that I might have to go away so that they can make me better... Chrissy's small face was crumpled and she was choking and spluttering the words out... And I DON'T want to live in a special school where I won't know anyone... By now the child was hysterical.

Hey, hey, now, said her father. Come here... and keep your head still, you'll hurt yourself.

No, I fucking won't. Fuck, fuck, fuck, fuckin no...

Calm down, honey, listen to your mum.

Miriam took her daughter's head between her hands and tried to stop the violent ticking back and forth, she lowered her hand under Chrissy's chin and drew her face to face, said: Look at me. Look at me and watch what I'm going to spell. Slowly, Miriam selected tiles while Chrissy shook and wept, and tried to run out of the room.

Gran said, Here now, Chrissy. Here, here, there's a good girl.

Miriam clicked the tiles into place, one after the other onto the board. You won't have heard or seen these words before, love, so watch me.

33

Ch-ck, ch-ck, said her daughter between her weeping. Tick-tick. Shit.

Stop crying, said her father. Please stop crying...

Miriam savoured the placing of each tile, click, click, click into place – TOURETTES SYNDROME.

Chrissy sniffed noisily and looked around, puzzled. Her father was smiling.

Bugger-shit.

You're not mad, Chrissy, said her mum. And you're not bad. Dr Moffat said they have a name for your condition, this disorder, and that is it. Look, *Tourette's Syndrome*. You're going to have treatment for this. You'll improve, we're sure, and you're not alone, they're discovering more and more children with it.

Chrissy still appeared puzzled.

This condition has been around for a hundred years, Chrissy, this syndrome – but it's only just been acknowledged as a treatable disorder! It's in its early stages but they're getting there. They really are.

Shit-bugger-damn, she spluttered. Will I have to go away?

NO, spelled her mother. NO.

Mourning Cloak

'It was 1945 when my baby girl was born. Such a long time ago isn't it?'

'It's not such a long time ago, Lili, not if you want to go back that far. Now, come along, let's get your hair brushed and you settled on those pillows, easy now, up we go… there.'

'Did I tell you about her? My little girl?'

'You did, Lili, but tell me again, I'm happy to hear as I tidy up…'

But of course the carer knew Mrs Liliana Pitowski would be asleep before she'd got beyond *'Oh, it was a hot, hot afternoon, and I could hear the bombs dropping all over London, even though she told me the war was over…'*

Liliana Pitowski slept a lot these days and was happier drifting back to meet her memories…

…It was a hot, hot afternoon, and I could hear the bombs dropping all over London, even though she told me the war was over. The din was dreadful, booming, banging and crashing and a lot of shouting in an excited kind of way. The 'angel of the street', I've forgotten her name (she wasn't a proper midwife but one of those souls that helped with births and the laying out of the dead, and I believe she helped women in the family way that didn't want to be in the family way), said the men *were* excited. Glad the war was over, and that they could earn a bit of government money making safe the buildings. Oh, the sight of those poor buildings, it made me weep.

'There's no need to cry Mrs Pitowski,' the angel had said, speaking slowly as if I was daft. Daft? I'm better educated than her that's for certain. I'm Polish, not daft!

'No bleedin' need at all if you just do as I say. And

35

remember' she said again, with deliberation, 'the war is over and you're a bit delirious that's all, so stop worrying about those bombs...' Then she screeched, 'Don't push, *now*, for Gawd's sake.' It seemed like only a minute before that she told me to push long and hard, and then after a while of cajoling, she suddenly said: 'Oh, my dear Lord, what have we got here in the Name of all that's Holy! I ain't seen one of these since, well... only seen one once before if truth were known – it's a bleedin' caulbearer! And I do not like it! I do not like it one bit, so I don't... And me on my tod! Hail Mary and Glory be to the Father. Just my luck! Bad luck, that I do know.'

I heard her snipping away. 'Well, I never did!' she said, and I could hear the distaste in her voice: 'It's a girl... I think it's a girl anyway... yes, a baby girl. Oh, my Lord, let's finish off and get out of here quick.'

Despite my state of confusion at the fuss the angel was making, I was aware of her speed. She gathered up her enamel bowls and threw in the scissors and a knife, and they clattered and sang with a kind of hysterical cacophony. She flung a towel over her shoulder as she scuttled away to empty the bowl of water. My baby, I thought, where is my baby? Just then there was another explosion from outside – the sound of more houses being razed to ground level; the rumbling went on and on in my head... then I heard the angel again as she flew in: 'I wish you'd not been in such an'urry Mrs Pitowski, so I don't.' Wiping her hands, she made towards the bottom of the bed, 'Why in Gawd's name you couldn't have gone full term like you was supposed to do, I do not know, then you could have had this up at the hospital!'

I tried to raise my head to see but by now, wrapped in a nice cloth, the bundle was thrust into my arms. 'There. There you are, she was in as much haste as you was. Didn't half slip out easy, her head covered in that caul.' Then the

36

angel of the street went as quick as if she were being chased by a devil.

I lay for ages with the bundle in my arms. Just her and me; she was quite, quite still and I could hardly see her breathing. The chaos outside had stopped for the evening and I remembered then that the war *was* over. And that my Motylosz would not be coming home. Ever. I was on my ow apart from my baby. The war took Motylosz in the last week of the fighting, and his mother with whom we lived, from influenza a year ago. These Pitowskis had been in Britain since the Great War saw them arrive: Motylosz's grandfather and grandmother – he always called them Dziadek and Babka no matter how anglicised he became, and his parents, Mama and Papa. That is what they all were to me: grandfather, grandmother, mother and father. My family, these four, and Motylosz, that's all I had. Now I am alone with only a baby, a baby who had been born to a strange reaction. I put her to my breast and she suckled.

Later, I noticed the caul-thing tossed carelessly behind, and saw it was as a chrysalis would be. An empty chrysalis. I did not think I could part with this strange item.

All things considered, I slept a beautiful sleep. I did not feel uncomfortable at all and was able to rise from my bed the next day, make a cup of tea, and see to my child. This is just as well because the angel of the street did not return, but sent a message with my landlady: *Please tell Mrs Pitowski I'm worn out, what with an up-all-night birth, and two old souls passing on – they need seeing to sharp, in this hot weather. Someone'll call in if she needs anything.* I wondered which of my neighbours had passed on? Was it Mr Wheelan? Mr Soyer? They were both very elderly and had not looked long for this world...

Anyway, to my child. My daughter. I was getting used to saying *my daughter*.

It was a new sound in my mind and I felt a fluttering in my stomach when I said it. Initially, I saw her features as mouse-like. Field-mouse-like. Her eyes were un-naturally bright for a new-born I thought, small, round and very open, and she had the palest covering of down on her tiny face. I'd heard this could occur in some cases, and soon disappear. I unwrapped the cloth; she had soiled herself of course, and so I gently lowered her into a nice roomy bowl and swished her little body with luke-warm water; her arms moved upwards in a kind of delight and to my surprise, I saw she had a fold of fine, fine skin under each arm, and when I turned her over, I saw they formed part of delicate wings. Not the feathery wings of a heavenly angel but folds of hardly discernible scaled skin. Butterfly wings. She was a butterfly! There was no mistaking it. I stroked the soft down on her silky back which I noticed tapered to a narrow tip, from which her legs moved uncertainly, as if she were trying them out for the first time at ballet class. I helped to dry her wings and saw there were two pairs on each side from her little hips reaching up to her shoulders. Finally dry, they looked beautiful.

I wanted to show off my daughter and so longed for my landlady to come in and see her, but she only hovered at the door and stretched her neck to appease me: 'She *is* a little thing isn't she, *quite* the tiny mite…' When I ventured out, street neighbours looked into the pram (it was a pushchair contraption with pink sides) to which I fitted a canopy, although the sunshine didn't seem to bother my baby's eyes at all. The neighbours were more curious than I would have expected. Hadn't they seen a new baby before? More than once, I wondered what that so-called midwife had told them about my en-caul birth. Oh, they are so superstitious these uneducated people!

Once I acknowledged that I had a winged creature for

my child, I bought a large, fitted fireguard so she could not be tempted to fly near the open flames. I bought a book called *A Photographic Guide of Butterflies of Europe and Beyond*, and started on page one. I found that butterflies were usually very beautiful, very pretty, and coloured beyond words. In my mind's eye, I could see fritillaries as *'intricate as a priceless masterpiece, with scaled wings of burnt orange and red, which can glow to dying embers as in a dog grate of coals: they could be as a jet of blue-yellow gas with a purple flame.'* Again in my mind's eye, I see the Whites and Yellows species as *'bone-white, green-veined, orange-tipped';* I could see *'brimstone and clouded-yellow, a delicate spot of lime, a splash of sunshine, a smudge of cold ashes.'*

But my child was not so well-appointed, not quite so pretty. Perhaps it was because her father, although very beautiful at times, could be more moth-like. Moths and butterflies are closely related in the order, Lepidoptera. Motylosz was rather pale-brown in his character, and instead of darting about, flitting from here to there, being inquisitive and adventurous as I, he tended to constantly be attracted to a singular bright light and made straight for it. He sported the slower, nocturnal behaviour of a moth and I have to admit, could be a pest at times. He must have seen something special in me because he said he had never felt comfortable with other girls.

Over the months, we got on very well, Mariposa and I. Mariposa is the Spanish word for butterfly. Why did I choose a Spanish name? I liked it. I could have chosen the Arabic, Yara, or Aldora which means 'winged gift', but I liked the sound of Mariposa Pitowski. It tripped off my tongue as a piece of music. And when I hummed and sang to my daughter, she practiced her ballet movements. Her arms were like another pair of legs, she used both sets of limbs as if she were anointing things so delicate was her touch as she went about the house, settling, rising, dancing from one colourful thing to another. I bought potted plants from the market, and created a miniature garden in the corner of the living room, with small stones and shells and a shallow dish of fresh water. The months turned into eighteen months and I saw that she grew no bigger. She was advanced in a quaint way of speaking and quite the young lady, preening herself as she looked at her reflection. I took out my sewing basket, riffled through my bag of material and created a lovely hooded cape for her which fell about her arms: it was designed to conceal her wings when we ventured out. I wasn't a very neat needlewoman but was proud of my effort. The material was rich velvet and the colour was a deep-purple-magenta. Between the layers, I sewed in the chrysalis-caul which I'd never had the heart to throw away.

I caught my daughter gazing out of the window and I said to her: 'Mariposa, my beautiful winged treasure, I sense that you would like to play outside, but it would not be safe in the yard. There are no flowers there to play on, no water to sip, no sunshine at the moment and *certainly* no MamaLili to brush you gently, to drip honey into your little mouth, and to sing to you.' Mariposa was such a dutiful child, she just smiled and said: 'You are correct MamaLili. There is nothing outside for me that I cannot have inside.'

I often consulted my book, *A Photographic Guide of Butterflies of Europe and Beyond,* and learned much with Mariposa perched near my shoulder; sometimes she pointed or alighted on a certain word or picture. Sometimes she gave a small sigh. On page twelve of the book, I found that the life span of a butterfly rarely went beyond a few weeks, many lasting only hours. It said: *No adult butterfly can live more than a year.* Oh my God! Oh my dear God! Mariposa was at that moment distracted by myriad, floating motes, so I quickly closed the page and said it was time for lunch. When she was dozing by the leaf of a huge aspidistra (which I had placed to form a small forest at the rear of the miniature garden), I sought out the page again, and tentatively looked at the words. I was heartened to read that there was one butterfly, just one, that could live for maybe a year: the *Mourning Cloak* or *Camberwell Beauty*. The illustrations were wonderful and showed this beauty in wings of rich velvet. The colour? A deep-purple-magenta.

The name *Mourning Cloak,* I read, is due to the appearance of the surface of the wings, said to resemble the traditional cloak worn by those in mourning, and which was sometimes draped over the casket of the deceased. *Mourning Cloaks* live for almost a year and are therefore among the most venerable of the Lepidopterans. My heart lifted. The negative piece of information might not be appropriate to us – Mariposa is already two years old and may have many more years with me. My stomach lurched as I read on: *when the time comes, all Lepidoptera become thin and frayed during their hibernation and migration; they die at last.*

Mariposa stayed with me for four years! One day, I found her tucked behind the aspidistra pot; she seemed petrified into immobility. She was totally still, looked a little thinner, and despite her wings being upright and touching as if in prayer, they appeared to be slightly frayed at the edges. I watched her for days, but I knew. Knew she had died at last.

She was so very light. Dried out. I placed her in a box lined with silk and over her, I lay her cape, her rich velvet cloak, the colour of deep-purple-magenta.

'Lili? Are you asleep?'

The carer touched her shoulder and heard a whisper:

'Oh did I drift off? Did you hear me tell you about my little girl?'

'I caught some of it, yes, of course I did. Would you like a drink?'

'Please get me some clear honey in warm water. Take your time, I'm in no hurry.'

Now, was that a butterfly on the windowsill? Lili watched through half closed eyes as first one, then two, winged creatures fluttered about uncertainly, both tentative as if they had not exercised their limbs for some time; both had downy covered bodies which quivered against the light. One with a modest cloak of milky-brown, and the other with wings the colour of deep-purple-magenta.

'Here you are, Lili,' said the carer. 'A nice glass of... Oh, Lili! Lili?'

First published in *Cautiously Tiptoeing... Out of the Light* Sept 2020

The Gold Coach

December 1953

Rachel Morris was fascinated by the shop window. She'd never noticed it before because her Mam wouldn't normally visit this run-down part of town, but since she'd gone to Secondary School, her world had widened. One day, meandering around the town, she'd found this place, and now, instead of dilly-dallying with her friends, she raced off as soon as she got out of the school gate and took this short detour, but always managed to get home on the dot of 3.45pm every day.

Here, most of the shops were empty in preparation for the local housing development, some boarded up already. But this one! This one appeared to have been freshly painted white; the windows were Georgian with bottle-bottom panes strategically placed, making the spotlight from within shine in a multi-faceted way. It was a Christmas window with small tufts of cotton-wool-snow stuck to the glass. The wide sill was full of toys: a clockwork skating rink set on a large mirror which this afternoon had three tiny skaters gliding about the snowflakes with their skirts flowing. Peg dolls, trumpets, water-colour paint sets, playing-cards, board-games, red and green baubles scattered about and umpteen gifts one might find in a Christmas stocking. In fact there was a filled stocking hanging up bulging with strange shapes. But Rachel only hankered after one thing in the window – the Coronation Gold Coach pulled by graceful-looking horses. She hoped she would get one for Christmas to go with all her other Royal memorabilia. The gold coach had the new, waving Queen Elizabeth II and the Duke of Edinburgh sitting inside.

The other thing which caught her eye more and more was the Santa Claus. He was leaning as if from a part of the shop she couldn't see because there was no light beyond the window. Life-size, Santa was on the left-hand side of the window and each day he seemed to be slightly different. He was dressed of course in a splendid costume with his thick white hair and beard just as she expected, but it was his smile. She put her head on one side and looked very closely. Surely he wasn't smiling that particular way yesterday. Today he seemed to smile with his eyes as well, crinkling them up in an inviting way. Come on in, they said in a kindly manner. But Rachel knew she couldn't, apart from having no money, she never had time to linger as her Mam was pretty strict. She found herself shyly waving her fingers at him and was certain she saw his fingers wiggle, too. See you tomorrow, his eyes said.

Rachel's Nainnie, Gwen, wound more protective cotton wool round and round until the parcel was twice its size, and addressed it: Mrs Wenna Morris, 31 Groes y Mynydd, Bangor. She added in capitals, NORTH WALES, in case the sorting office in Chester didn't know where Bangor was, and as it was getting close to Christmas with all the mail to-ing and fro-ing it could easily get lost. It was the first time for many years since she'd not spent Christmas with them, but no-one wants a bronchial cough around them on Christmas Day, do they? Anyway, she thought, I'm bound to be better in a couple of weeks but until then, this is the best I can do. She'd popped in a note saying: *Tell Lena and Tom not to call – I don't want them catching what I've got. Love, Mam xxx* Inside the box, which held a replica of the Coronation Gold Coach complete with horses, she wrote to her granddaughter: *Nainnie's got more to go with this when she sees you. A surprise! Have a lovely time with everyone on the 25th xxxxxx*

All Gwen's family, well, the women anyway, were obsessed with the Royal Family. Over the years Gwen had accumulated a large collection of paraphernalia: magazines, and picture-books charting the childhood of both princesses, Elizabeth and Margaret Rose, commemorative issues of Elizabeth's wedding in 1947, cups and wall plates and other little mementoes. And when King George VI died, well, Gwen's mountain of memorial newspapers took on new heights.

This year, Gwen decided that all her collection should go to Rachel. Now. No point in waiting until I've passed on, she thought. It will give her a wonderful boost to her very own collection of Royal mementos, and one day, might be worth a fortune. She spent a nice afternoon getting the books together and choosing the best selection of newspaper cuttings and special editions. She kept the ornaments for now though – the place would be bare without them.

The time went by quickly as she packed up the magazines, pausing every couple of minutes to gaze once again at the lovely, perfect-looking Royal family. It didn't seem long since His Majesty had died, and she still felt the shock of it.

Gwen filled one box, tied it with string, and wrote 'For Rachel, from Nainnie'. The second box, she left open, because she anticipated *The Bangor Chronicle*'s special pull-out depicting what the new Queen and the Duke of Edinburgh, would likely be doing as they spent their first Christmas together in this role, in Auckland, New Zealand, where they were on a six-month tour of the Commonwealth. She wondered what it would be like to spend Christmas in the warm weather, and who would be looking after Prince Charles and Princess Anne, and if they would miss their parents on Christmas Day?

She placed the scrap in – her most prized treasure –

45

leaving space for *The Bangor Chronicle's* 'Royal Christmas Edition'.

Rachel's, parents, Wenna and Edward, were looking forward to Christmas with her brother, Tom and his wife, Lena. They'd written to say that they would travel by train on Christmas Eve afternoon from Colwyn Bay, bringing with them, Tom's mother-in-law, June. It would be June's first Christmas without her husband and Wenna wanted it to be special for her. There were a few more things to sort out but she was well organised.

'Goodness me! Where *is* Rachel?' Wenna looked at the clock. It was nearly 5pm. 'She should have been home an hour ago.' It was the last day of school before they broke up for the holidays.

Rachel was determined to have one last peek at the window. One last, longing look at the gold coach, hoping and crossing her fingers that it would be hers on Christmas morning. Up against the cotton wool snowflakes, Rachel's face looked disappointed. The coach had gone. Oh, no! She raised her hand to her forehead and scrutinised the sill again as if she were looking out to sea.

She felt silly as her eyes swam with tears. I'm twelve years old she said to herself. Stop being such a baby. A movement to the left made her look at Santa. He appeared different again this afternoon. A wide smile, a finger beckoning, and tantalisingly showing from the top of his laden sack – the coach! It was shining more golden that she had ever imagined. So it was for her, then. He'd kept it for her!

December 1996

After Gwen died aged ninety-three, Wenna asked Tom and Lena if they would clear out Mam's house. I can't face it, she'd told them.

Nothing much in the home had changed in over forty years, except that Gwen had got rid of the Royal mementos from the front parlour. Tom smiled when they eventually got to the spare bedroom and found them all individually wrapped up in newspaper and nestling in one of the cardboard boxes.

'I suppose these might be worth something today,' Lena said.

'I suppose,' said Tom. 'We'll take them to the auction room with the furniture.'

He prised open the top of a box and coughed at the dust it raised. All his mother's Royal paraphernalia: the newspapers yellowed and brittle to the touch, and the scrapbook choc-a-bloc with Coronation pictures. *The Bangor Chronicle* lay next to it. Tucked inside, the 'Royal Christmas' pull-out didn't look as if it had ever been opened.

In 1996, the *Chronicle's* 1953 front page, still had the awful power to shock, with the words: 'Where is twelve-year-old Rachel Morris? Last seen at about 4pm on the afternoon of Monday Dec 21st peering intently into the window of Lewis's Hardware store in run-down lower Bangor. The store had been vacant for over six years and the window held nothing but miscellaneous rubbish.'

———————

First published in *Cautiously Tiptoeing… Into the Thirteen Days of Christmas* Dec 2020

Mothers and Fathers

I had two mothers and two fathers. When I was a seven-year-old I thought that was unfair because Gill Waterstone only had one father and no mother at all, and James Jackson only had one mother.

Of course, neither went to our church *Our Lady of the Rosary*, as we did; my mum, dad and sister, so didn't even know the father guardian, Father Ethelbert, or our mother superior, Mother Providence. Charged with our spiritual welfare, both were diligent and sincere, and I took in every word. Armed with the sign of faith, Mother Providence wore her Rosary and Cross at her breast. Father Ethelbert's wooden Rosary was tied around his waist. His brown, hooded habit made me think of Friar Tuck except that our friar was lean. I loved the way his habit hung and swished with an authoritative sound as he walked. When he was home at the Friary, he wore sandals on his bare feet; they smacked the tiled floor as he came to answer the bell.

Mother Providence was corvid-like; long, black, head-veil and gown over her white wimple from which her beaky nose peeped. Black shoes. When I was seven, I thought Mother Providence was over a hundred-years old because her bony fingers looked like dried twigs. These she poked around inside a large glass jar to loosen the pear-drops she dished out every Saturday morning if we had been good in Catechism. Each week she said, Off you go and play in the grounds for ten minutes; come back when I ring the bell. One week she withheld the sweets because we dilly-dallied too long. I remember watching her from behind a tree, her figure bent as she stood in the doorway shaking the little bell, its querulous tinkling lost in the air at *Tan y Foel* Convent.

The nuns were lovely to us. But one of them was

stealing our cocoa. Mixed with sugar in a jar, the cocoa lived in a tall cupboard. At 10.30am, a spoonful was added to hot water and milk for our morning drink. Arthur James pencil-marked the label every week to see if any was missing, and often there was. Peter Brook said he was going to tell Father Ethelbert when he came to give us extra lessons, but I don't think he ever did because we were all a bit afraid of the father guardian. He arrived dressed as he did when he was out to business: a black suit with Roman collar, a black trilby hat, shiny black brogues, and a brown briefcase. Once he opened the briefcase and it held a railway timetable and an apple.

Mother Superior never went out to business.

Not a month went by without Father Ethelbert telling us of the unrepentant man on his deathbed. Unrepentant to his last breath. I was left shuddering at that dying man's audacity and wondered if the thieving nun would confess her cocoa sin before she died.

_____

First published online by Bridge House Publishing's *CaféLit* in February 2020, with a slightly different title

Mitzi

Mitzi's eyes opened slowly but she couldn't see a thing beyond the blanket. Although she was naked, she was warm and just wanted to go back to sleep. She shifted a little. Over the years she'd been used to hearing the muffled clank, the soporific hum, the throaty gurgle of trapped air and water as the old pipes tried to keep the temperature constant, but that only had the effect of sending her back to doze again under her covers.

Little happened down here in the cellar these days. She was bored. And she was very lonely. Sometimes to relieve her boredom she shifted her position so that she lay down on the flat rocks and let the sun touch her all over. There she listened to the sea whispering along the tiny beach and shielded her eyes to watch a bird or a goat. Lying there it was easy to drift off as the waves lapped. That's where she was when she awoke this very afternoon.

She became aware of a diffused light through her thick covering. A light and a moving shape. Three shapes. Two women and a man approached the hangers and started to manhandle her.

'Steady on,' one of the women said. 'Carefully does it.'

It took Mitzi a little while to ascertain that she was not dreaming one of her long, long dreams and that the people were actually here in the cellar. Alarmed, she rolled over and eased herself back into her sitting position on the rocks. She pulled the picnic rug around her left thigh, she shook her fair, bobbed hair. Settled, she gazed out to sea. The voices came and went as their owners moved around trying to get a good hold on her frame. She recognised that these were people she knew nothing of. Her mind raced in all directions, and very soon she was back at the beginning. Or was it one of the ends?

She could remember being brought here, her and some of the others: the blind child, Sukie, London Lily and Bessie Devay (Bessie always got her full name). She remembered they'd been crated up after Harro died and placed in the depth of a big building; she'd heard the sounds echoing as they'd been carried through various sized rooms, heard the footsteps descending into a cellar-type place. They'd been wrapped and strapped into position never to see the light of a real day since. Mitzi'd heard the others talking periodically and didn't like the sound of Miss Freida Jenkins shouting, 'Where am I? Where am I? Where are you all?'

At the time, Mitzi had not known where she was; the others sounded just as lost as they called out to one another; she had been struck dumb with shock for a while but one or two of the others cried pitifully. After that, she hadn't seen her friends again. She'd heard things though; she remembered girls calling out down there, very young voices there in the dark with the older women trying to comfort them saying: 'Sshhh, quiet, quiet…' She heard men too; she could hear their thick pint glasses on a table and the click of dominoes and the flick of cards. She could smell pipe tobacco. Her ears had been awake when she was, but her eyes were not so acute.

As her senses now returned, Mitzi heard these voices quite clearly. Through her covering, she recognised that the words spoken by these people were delivered in an unfamiliar manner somehow, as if from another age. She recognised animation in their voices as they began to move her. 'Careful… steady on now… steady on.'

Mitzi Cavell had been dead for almost ninety years. She'd died young of consumption. It was all that damp living, and living as if there were no consequences. Mitzi never cared about a proper roof over her head or if her bed was aired.

The people worked with the careful reverence acquired from many years devoted to the handling of paintings. Mitzi's frame was manoeuvred down from the stacks, placed in a wheeled carrier and taken through to another room where the restorers waited to assess the works. Here, they slowly, even seductively lowered the covering to the sound of gasps as her bare shoulders were exposed, then her breasts.

'Oh my God! Just look at the flesh tone against the granite. It's exquisite!'

'And the colours of the sea…'

They spoke to each other as if Mitzi wasn't in the room – as if she wasn't sitting a foot away from them! She frowned and pouted like a child, apprehensive and uncomfortable amidst these people. She was also now chilly in this atmosphere. Mitzi was used to the brisk sea air on her skin but this air was dry and not at all sympathetic. Her hair needed a wash, her lips needed oil and her body needed the soothing strokes of the softest brush Harro had in his jug.

She lowered her eyes against it all, disoriented. Back in the past where she felt she belonged, Mitzi heard shells and little pebbles run up the sand, and fall back, quietly, hopelessly, only to try again. She heard the birds calling and the goats shifting stones as they tip-toed on the hillside. She heard Harro whistling a tuneless tune as he put out his brushes, introduced thick coils of raw umber, rose-madder and yellow ochre to his palette. She saw him pour pure turps, and fetch rags. She saw him puff up his chest and call out saying: 'I'm ready! Are y'decent?' And she heard his wife, Isoline, say in the background: 'Oh, must you shout so!' And then under her breath, 'There's no show without Punch.'

Isoline was a potter. Made vases and pots of an orangey colour, and dishes, too. In earthenware, she created a strange combination of swollen-chested birds and sinewy cats. She was as good an artist as her husband, but hadn't his charisma. It was hard to tell whether it was pride or irritation when she inevitably and often declared when he was showing off: *There's no show without Punch!*

Once uncovered, Mitzi felt exposed in every sense of the word and looked around for a familiar face; she looked for Harro. He would know what to do, but he was not here. Her lip quivered. The light hurt her eyes and made them weep. Harro was not here, and she was anxious.

While she'd been asleep in her rack Mitzi often dreamed of Harro, a larger-than-life persona, who was also her surrogate father. He who promised her mother that he and Isoline would take care of her – Mitzi being only seventeen. She'd dreamed of Rosie and the deserted cottages, the little winding track, the waves, and flotsam and jetsam that came and went in the abandoned, village colony. How could she not? she asked herself. How could the sight of Rosie washing herself outside the makeshift hut on the cliffs leave her? How could she ever forget the sight of Harro standing not far away at his easel, pipe in his mouth, hat always at that silly angle, painting swiftly as if at any moment, Rosie should disappear over towards Llantir where her unsuitable lover lived? How could she not smile each time she heard Harro singing in his deep off-key voice, each time he recited lines of obscure poetry with a pint glass in his hand in the pub or at the studio parties with everyone hanging on his every and last word, and Isoline, saying under her breath: 'Why must he be so loud?' and again, *'There's no show without Punch!'* And how could she forget the sight of Rosie's bruised body after it was found, strangled by her lover and left under a wildflower hedge while everybody thought she'd gone home to nurse her father? And Bessie Devay – oh, Bessie, those perfect, delicate wrists and slender ankles of yours! Everyone wanted to paint you, Bessie Devay, but Harro nearly always bagged you first!

Mitzi was frightened. Her sudden departure from the depth of yesterday and all that was familiar to her tore at her heart. Her thoughts went this way and that and got lost. Why was she awakened now in this place? Out of kilter with yesterday and overlapping into today. She sighed, her fear fluttering like so many feathers in her stomach. She didn't belong here with real people. She closed her eyes and let the tears run down her dry and cracked cheeks. They snapped open again. The people were talking about Harro. One of the curators told a young assistant that there was a huge resurgence and interest in the 'Porthnant School', the artist colony founded by Harold Mostyn.

She grew tired, her eyelids closed. She was glad when they said it was time to pack up for the weekend. She settled back, covered herself and soon found herself returned to Porthnant, the tiny abandoned quarrying village in North Wales, and the artists who worked there for almost twenty years. With her mind all over the place, she remembered dying and the raw pain in her chest. It had taken her weeks to die as she wasted away, her lungs wheezing and exploding in sudden bursts. Oh, dear, the others must be dead too after all this passed time.

Unsettled, she wriggled her shoulders. One of the labels at the back of her frame was coming loose and it irritated her. She reached for it; it was crinkly with age: *Mitzi on Porthnant Rocks. Malvern City Art Gallery 1956 – 40gns.* Eagerly now she eased the other labels off. An older one: *The Tremarl Gallery, Cardiff 1942. The Royal Cambrian Academy 1950.* And the most recent, *The Royal Academy 1960 – 100 gns.*

Oh, what was that? A rustling and a clambering and a voice she thought she'd never hear again.

'You aint 'alf suffered, Mitzi Cavell! Where's that warm glow gone? That smooth body you once had? That shining hair?'

'Lily?' Mitzi's eyes scrunched up. 'Lily!'

'Who else?' said the dark-haired girl, her creamy-brown legs straddling a fallen branch and her reaching up to pick blackberries from the hedgerow.

'Oh, Lily where have you been all this time? Where did you go? You disappeared so quickly we didn't say goodbye.'

'I know, Mitzi. I was sold about a year after we came here – been back in London all this time, same old family, same house, same walls. I'm thrilled to have a change of scene.' They looked at one another and Lily said, 'Stop crying y'daft ha'porth.'

'I can't help it, Lily'

'Come 'ere m'darling… you always was the baby of us all…'

Mitzi slid into Lily's frame and they hugged and cooed over each other.

'Hello, you two!'

They both spun round.

'I have to agree you need a bit of looking after, Mitzi. You'll be as good as new once they've finished with you…'

'Rosie! You're here too?'

'Course I am,' she said from within her frame.

'Where've you been, Rosie?'

'All over the place. Moved a lot, ended up not far from here… Been taken care of quite well, but you Mitzi, you need a clean… O, don't start crying again, I'm just teasing you.'

Lily wiped Mitzi's cheek and they looked over to where

Rosie sat with a posh hat on in the corner of the dark snug, and they started to laugh: they laughed and laughed hysterically and eventually squealed with joy.

'Come over here you two, there's more room and maybe Evsie'll get us a drink... You still take a drop of gin, Lily?' Rosie moved up and made room and they hugged and hugged, and Evsie brought them drinks.

'D'you think there're more of us? Here? Down here?'

'Of course y'silly girl.' Rosie stroked Mitzi's sun blanched hair. 'We're here for Harold's retrospective. Let me show you who else's arrived...'

'Oh, you mean...?'

Rosie, who was always theatrical, threw her arm out, 'Roll up Roll up Ladies and Gents – cast your eyes this way.'

Gypsy Tad and Queenie stood in front of a tent. Tad's grin crinkled up the sides of his face, showing faint crackle in his cheeks. Mitzi tumbled out of Rosie's frame: 'Tad! You're here, and Queenie! Queenie, you beauty, you beautiful girl, you. Oh, your mouth is still so, so soft.' She nuzzled into the horse's face. All the while, Boxer and Monty ran round and round Queenie's legs barking and yelping. 'I can't believe it's you, Tad!' Mitzi had never felt happier. 'Who else's here, Tad? Who else?'

'Most of us.'

'Really and truly?'

'Really and Truly.'

'You mean those who left us? Those who were sold?'

'Yes.'

'What about my mother?'

'She's here too.'

'Oh. Oh, my!'

Her mother, **Connie, the Seamstress**, sat at the window. Her charcoal grey dress hung in many tones from the light;

her cobwebby white collar and cuffs were as fresh as the day she was painted. Her mother smiled at her as if to say, Let's finish off your sampler! And Mitzi saw the green and red and blue hieroglyphs of thread weaving 'A's and 'B's and 'C's, and numbers up to ten. And a Bible quote and her birth date of January 15th 1898.

Mitzi turned, bewildered, as everyone started up again. Suddenly.

'Sshhh.'

'What?' Mitzi said. 'What?' she asked again, childlike, giggling.

'Can't you hear?'

'Hear, what?'

'Listen.' Lily and Rosie looked at each other and Lily winked.

Mitzi pouted. 'I can hardly hear anything above this noise, it's all a muddle of voices and hooves and shouts and animals. Hush, Boxer, and you Monty, for goodness sake stop barking. Tad stop them!' She turned to the four old men in the pub. 'And you,' she said. 'Less racket, please. How can you make so much din when all you're doing is playing dominoes?'

Gypsy Tad quietened down the dogs and the men stopped playing to draw long on their pints.

A kind of quiet settled and Mitzi inclined her head at Rosie who said: 'Can't you hear? Can't you hear, Isoline?'

'Isoline?'

'Yes. Listen, child. Look!' Rosie placed her hands either side of Mitzi's face and turned her towards the dark doorway. 'Look.'

A lantern bobbed its way out of the shadows and there, Isoline and Harro emerged slowly towards them. Isoline was talking and smiling up at him, and Harro was shaking his head.

'Well I never. Well I never,' he kept saying. 'Just look at you all.'

Everyone ran towards the couple, and started to talk at once.

Mitzi, dumbstruck for a full fifteen seconds, could not contain her weeping. She flew towards Harro and could hear Isoline saying, 'Here he is. Here he is. *There's no show without Punch!'*

First published in *Cautiously Tiptoeing... Out of the Light* Sept 2020

Family Ties

Uncle Ernie and Aunt Margery were very close. First cousins in fact. They lived in a nice area on the Wirral. We lived in North Wales and they loved to visit. They used to stay with us but soon preferred a self-catering cottage or apartment, one near the beach so they could give Pip the run of it. Margery called Ernie, Ernest, and Ernie called her Jerry. When I was a small child, I thought they were one and the same person with their features being alike; Ernie had a delicate facial structure feature and hair that grew over his ears; Margery had a 'short back and sides' and it shone with a touch of Brylcreem, like my dad's did.

Each year they bought a new piece of holiday clothing, and once they were satisfied with their purchases, gave a piece away. I remember Margery instigating the purchase of a pair of canvas shoes for Ernie and insisted he donated his comfy leather sandals to the jumble sale; he hobbled for the rest of the week. That year she bought a pair of striped slacks for herself, navy and white. She would not go out until she'd sewn up the hems by three inches. She was very short in height, and Ernie was over six feet tall, but he was no match for Margery and had to wait until almost lunch-time before they could 'take the air'.

When they stayed with us, they brought their own teapot, a stainless steel one that could sit on the stove to keep the tea hot for their second cup, which was always drunk with a Marie biscuit. Their tea also came with them, mixed three-to-one Ynnan China with Earl Grey in a Twinings Anniversary tea caddy (1706-1981).

The last year they came, we were invited to visit them in their 'Cottage by the Sea' in Criccieth. I saw the same teapot under a low light, and the caddy just at arm's length. I noticed that neither Uncle Ernie nor Aunt Margery sported anything new. And for the first time, I thought their faces looked worn. Pip had never been replaced.

I recalled these things vividly when Aunt Margery died and at the funeral, someone mentioned in a hushed tone that Uncle Ernie's father had been more than over-fond of Aunt Margery's mother in the early 1930s. I said I wanted to hear what they were saying and that's when it dawned on me how close they really were.

The Crowman

Heini Mostyn turned into the One Stop and made his way
around the back where the place boasted Two Rooms to
Let. Girlie needed a night's rest on some good hay and the
cart needed a few planks securing. Heini'd seen the sign
two days ago, 'Benefit Way', with an appendage: 'On route
to Mount Misery 150 miles. Via Opportunity. State of
Texas'. And under that, someone had pinned a board and
scrawled in scattered letters: *'theres plenty more routes
bettern this un.'* He recalled laughing and saying, 'Hey,
Girlie, let's take the Benefit Way'; and so they had, seeing
little of interest in the wide fields and scattered homesteads
until scarecrows started appearing on the roadside. All
pointing the way he was going. He was amused when he
noticed one scarecrow had been turned to point directly into
the One Stop.

The old man leaned out of the stable door at the rear of
the store. He looked as if he'd shrunk out of his Texas
Ranger hat.

'Come on in, youngster, and I'll deal with you sooner'n
you can say poison snakes… Loosen up her tack,' he said
nodding to the horse. 'And there's water at the trough.
Y'might have to pump it some.'

'Thank you, sir.'

'You sure welcome, boy… Come round the front when
you're done.'

The store was full of hope for the traveller: water,
packed savouries, fancy cakes, bottled gas, toiletries,
postcards, mail services (limited). Animal feed was stacked
next to an arrow pointing to The Rest Room & Mini-Thrift;
and the sign again: Two Rooms to Let.

'I'll take a room if that's all right.'

''Tain't much to it.'

61

'Has it got a shower?'

'Has Rose Kennedy got a black dress?' the old man spluttered and his lungs crackled in secret mirth as if he was the first to say such a thing. 'And a tee-vee, though you have to pay extra. Slot. Folks like you usually want a repair station.'

'Pardon?'

'Somewhere to fix up all that's broke on your wagon.'

'Ah, quite right. You have such a place.'

'Just to the left. It's bit extra though.'

'I have my own tools but I'll take advantage of the offer. Thank you.'

'You from someplace else?'

'I suppose so, yes.'

'Not from Ameriky.' It was a statement.

'No, sir. From Great Britain. The United Kingdom.'

'What's great about it? What's united in it?'

'Well…'

The old man's rheumy eyes looked as if he awaited a revelation; his open mouth exposed a wet cave.

'You're not familiar?'

The eyes and mouth did not move.

'With the United Kingdom? England…?'

'Oh,' said the old man, letting out a breath. 'That place.'

'And Scotland, Ireland and Wales. United countries. I come from Wales.'

'Never heard'n it. Let's settle up shall we.

Girlie stood under the shelter as Mostyn, as he liked to be known, was still smiling at the old man calling him a young man. He was almost forty years old. He inspected Girlie's feet and shoes, brushed her down, and led her to a stable of sorts where the eventual sound of her munching and chewing feed was comforting.

His intention to travel by car had been halted a month ago when he'd seen the two young girls at the side of the road with Girlie and the cart and a cardboard For Sale sign. He'd bought the whole contraption. The girls said they'd changed their minds and were going back home. Their eyes told him something else; a man stood nonchalantly against a smart vehicle a few yards away. The girls did not answer Mostyn when he asked what the horse was called. He dealt with the hire car and transferred his stuff: bedding, writing materials, a camera, some tinned food and bottled water. So much for driving, he'd thought – whizzing from place to place had not been the best way to chat to the natives. He soon learned that wandering along off a beaten track took him to poor places where he inveigled himself into the lives of folk who didn't know they had stories to tell – some true and some made up just for the glee of the teller having someone to listen. There were rich pickings on the smaller dirt roads and tracks. He wasn't heading for anywhere in particular.

He set to checking over his cart at the repair station; re-arranged things a bit, shook the blanket and aired the bedding, tightened up the tarpaulin that served as his roof, and filled up his water tank. He hammered home the loose wood and tested everything by shaking and prodding. Satisfied, he stood awhile outside; strolled to the front of the store. The heat bore down and the quiet was deafening. A few cars went by. One stopped, and he saw the old man fill her up and serve the woman with bottled water, packaged food, and a four-foot statue of Padre Pio from the Mini-Thrift.

Mostyn bought a cold beer and in the strange violet of the early evening light, sat on the wood bench and looked as far as his eye could see. The area was flat and parched. Wind-pumps against the sky. Grain elevators. There was a kind of lonely despair about it, wide and empty except for the ribbon of a dirt road. He saw choreographed crows gracing a sky the colour of lavender; they circled over the arid plains of the Texas panhandle.

'Don't be fooled,' the old man said, creeping up on him. 'There's plenty going on out there…' and sat himself down with a resigned sigh. The wide silence got louder, and they sat. The lazy tune of toad-croak and cicadas was soothing and soporific.

A farmhand turned in towing a trailer that looked as if it desperately needed the repair station.

'Ah, here's Dowdy Wilson. 'Bout time he come and showed me the colour of his money. Hey, there Dowdy.'

'Evenin' Ol' Man.'

'What can I get ya'?' The old man strolled over, tipping his hat back.

'Need feed.'

'Got y'purse with y'?'

'Some…'

'Some's better'n none I s'pose.'

Mostyn watched him load up the feed, saw cash changing hands and smiled as he saw the old man licking his pencil and making laborious notes in a dirty, tan leather-bound book. I bet there's some stories in that book, he mused.

On a billboard, a gaudy poster advertised 'Opportunity's Spring Fete: Stalls, Bric-a-Brac. The Freakiest Freak Show You Ever Did See' and 'The Popular Scarecrow Competition'. The One Stop window was full of Wanted and For Sale cards, some to 'take away NOW', enticed in faded green magic-marker. Mostyn looked at the cards behind various shades of sticky-tac: Hutches and Pens going cheap due to fever-flu. Bag of infant clothes. Rooster and lady hens wanted. Dirty Thief stole my daughter's Try-Cycle Help me

Catch Him. Callipers and a crutch for sale (no longer required. Mamie Lang R.I.P.) The cards spoke volumes to him; they were rich in stories: just what he was after – the tales hidden behind the words. The pictures he conjured up took him behind closed doors and half-open curtains into kitchens and bedrooms. Behind sheds. Then, MISSING. $15,000 Reward for the safe return of Alice-May Locke. Aged sixteen. Last seen November 12th, 1972. Five feet, three inches tall, grey-blue eyes, corn-coloured shoulder-length hair. Last seen wearing red plaid slacks, matching jacket, black ankle-boots. A three-string pearl necklace.

Yes, plenty of material in the window to fill more than one collection of short fiction. He'd soon learned that not every reader liked happy-ever-after endings.

He bought a steak and kidney pie in a round tin to eat later.

Y'can eat here,' said the old man. 'There's a portable oven you can heat things up in and I'd be obliged if you'd share a beer with me.' Mostyn smiled; he was sure he heard him murmur as he turned towards the shelves. ''Course, that'll be a bit extra…'

'You live here? Above the shop so to speak?'

'Sure do. Constant. You never know who or what comes 'long…'

'You were a Ranger?' Mostyn said, looking at the old man's head. 'You must have some stories to tell…'

'No-o-sir. Found this here hat in the Thrift Room.'

'Ah-ha.'

'You never know what fetches up here.'

'I'll stretch my legs and take you up on your offer about supper time. Thanks.'

Mostyn walked off the road for about a half mile. He realised he was in a kind of hamlet, with farms and a few homesteads spread over some miles. In the far distance he saw a low-lying house surrounded by small fields, one cultivated green, one yellow, and two the pale brown of ploughed earth. Another field looked like a junk yard sporting abandoned cars and trucks and outbuildings. He saw a movement and watched a woman with a stick cajole a few cattle somewhere else, and a man come at her, also wielding a stick. Later, he questioned the old man.

'That's my neighbour. Josephine Newcome and her no-good son-of-a-bitch son,' he said.

The old man had laid up a pull-down board that served as his table. Tin plates, tin mugs for tea and glass jars for the beer. Forks. 'They live in the nearest farm, about a mile away. Keep theirselves to theirselves – Hmm… Next town's not far away, a few miles yonder; s'called Opportunity. And so it goes on in every which-way direction.' He switched on the oven and Mostyn could smell stale fat and felt a taste of it in his mouth.

'You alone in the world, boy?'

'Me? No, no. Not at all.'

The old man looked quizzically at him. 'How come you alone then?'

'Ah, it's no mystery. I'm working.'

'Working.' The old man's expression did not change.

'Yes. I'm a writer.'

'A writer, eh?'

'Yes. Of short stories.'

The old face showed no sign of understanding. 'You call that work, do ye? Real work with cash coming in.'

'Yes. It's not as easy as it sounds, though.'

'You one a'them beatnik-hippies?'

Mostyn chuckled. 'No, I'm a just a boring chap. Married, two children.'

'And that wife a'yours don't mind you travelling all over the Texas panhandle getting up to no good mischief?'

66

Mostyn, still smiling, shook his head.

'So that's the new way is it… it beats me and I don't mind saying!'

'I'd like to know what the story is around here? How come you set up the One Stop?'

Fuelled by whisky and beer, the old man explained that this was to have been a boom town area with hog farms galore, houses, plenty a'work and big opportunities for those who 'foresaw'. He said the company that planned the hog farms was Big Business. A lot of people had had their fingers in the pie so to speak, and he broke off to laugh at his own joke. 'Sure, a lot of folks stood to gain a whole load-a-cash. Me included. See, by then I'd already bought this place, just coupla miles on the outskirts of Opportunity, thinking I'd struck gold…' The old fella suckled the bottle of Jack Daniels as if he were at his mother's breast, and offered it to Mostyn. Mostyn lifted up his beer and intimated, *I'm fine with this*, and with a nod of his head, encouraged, *carry on, I'm listening.*

'Yes, sir, we all stood to make a packet.' He flicked his hat to the back of his head and went on. 'But some son-of-a-bitch gov'ment official, set to make his own killing, put a stop to the hog farms saying the stink of hogs and their muck'd drive away the rich folks he wanted to build houses for up on the higher plains. Greedy mother-fucker. This place coulda been rolling in money for ever'one! Jobs for tannery workers, meatpackers, canning factories, you name it… And now all we got is a wasteland 'cause he didn't even build his fancy houses. He got his comeuppance, so help him, sure to God!' Then he stopped to catch his breath, re-positioned his hat and tried to find the loose end to his story.

'What happened to him? The mother-fucker of a government official?'

'Well.'

There was the sound of some bug circling the light and the old man took a swipe at it; the lampshade swung in a drunken dance sending the light into all the grimy corners of the shack-like room.

'Is there more to the story?'

'Ah. Rose Kennedy again...' and he croak-chuckled from somewhere deep in his scrawny chest. The old man spent some time regaining his breath. As the light settled again, the buzz continued.

Mostyn reached into the table-fridge and opened another bottle of beer. The old man held his glass out too, and sat sipping his beer, alternately sucking at Jack Daniels.

'Well. As I was sayin'. As I was sayin'... that man got the biggest comeuppance of all time.'

'He did?'

'So bad he gave up the building when the foundations had just been set. Never went near the site again.'

'What happened?'

'His daughter.'

'His daughter?'

'Yes. His only child. That girl was barely sixteen, a whole rich future ahead of her.'

'What happened?' asked Mostyn, quietly.

The old man slapped his hand down on the table. 'Nobody knows.'

'What?'

'Vanished. Disappeared off the face of the earth. The gov'ment man put up thousands and thousands a'dollars reward. But no sign. Ever.'

'What did the rangers think?'

'Them? What could they think only that someone who had a finger in the sausage and pork pie business was teaching him a lesson? And let me tell you there were

68

plenty a'those. Plenty who had their own lives turned upside down. Kaput!'

Mostyn was shaken up. 'That's bad', he said. 'That's bad. When did all this happen?'

'Four years back in '72. Could'a been yesterday. He's gone mad, the gov'ment man. In a straight-jacket I heard.'

'I'm not surprised.'

'No, sir. No sir-ree. Still puts up the reward though. Still stands. His lawyer replaces the posters ever six months and puts notices in the newspapers ever month. Looky here…' and he withdrew some faded and wind-beaten posters. The girl looked out, her face open and confident. Mostyn read the same words that were on the window poster, and pictured Alice-May Locke in her red plaid slacks and her black ankle boots. And her pearl necklace. $15,000 Reward…

Suddenly Mostyn felt weary.

'That's not a good story, sir. I'm sorry to hear it.'

'No indeedy, youngster, No indeed. 'Course, she ain't the only young girl to vanish in these parts…'

Mostyn rose early, purchased stock to take away, packed it in a sturdy larder-box and by six-thirty returned onto Benefit Way. He was on the road again.

'You call back now,' ordered the old man, no sign of a hangover.

'Certainly will, sir. If I come this way again.' He and Girlie moved off in the direction of Mount Misery with the intention of stopping at Opportunity with its freak show. Two miles along and he knew he was getting near as he saw the scarecrows again; lifeless bodies hooked over fences, some nailed to telegraph poles or tied to moth-eaten chairs. Soon, Mostyn saw the marquee and smaller tents and caravans taking over a huge field. Pens were being staked out and hot-dog vans were vying for space. Opportunity was one of the bigger towns he'd come across. Two schools, junior and senior high, large hardware store, cafés and a diner, houses offering 'bed and board' and two small hotels. Two banks, a shave'n'barbers, a Salvation Army Thrift store. Washerette. An Episcopal church and a Baptist Prayer House. A gaming house and a disguised whore-house called Y'Comfort Stop. A courthouse. On the street corner a woman dressed as a ring-master shouted, 'Stalls, Bric-a-Brac, Barb-Bee-Qu, Games, Sports, Fancy Dress and The Biggest and Best Scarecrow Competition to be judged by the Crowman, A-aabe Lincoln-Nance.' This announcement was heralded by the push of a button somewhere in her pocket, and an off-key musical fanfare. 'A-aaand,' the ringmaster hollered in colourful tones, 'T'say nothin' of the Fort-uuune Teller and the Freak Sho-ooooow!' She cracked her whip and sent it swirling round and over her head. 'There's plenty opportunities in Opportunity tomorrow. Roll up, roll up, I won't tell you turkey-critters again.'

There were so many scarecrows that Abe Lincoln-Nance started judging that day. He carried a notebook and could be seen tugging and pulling the fence-hung, the crucified and the resting effigies along the roadside. Then he made for the gardens, the park and the school playground. Saturday morning came and he demonstrated a continued, obsessive interest in the crow-scarers on the Fete field itself. He was a first-class scarecrow maker. Farmers bought new ones every year, especially since Abe started inserting battery-worked and mechanical parts that lifted and waved arms in a jerky movement; 'See them crows fly off to hell 'n' back!' he said when his latest creation doffed his bowler and let out a screech.

Abe Lincoln-Nance wore a tall black opera hat, and for

all the world looked like a scarecrow himself Mostyn thought, as he followed him round and made his own notes. Sure there's stories here, even if it's only from the clothes the scaremongers wore: two guys dressed in wedding suits; they were decorated with feathers stuck fast to black tar. A buxom maid was kitted out in bobby-socks, pumps and a schoolgirl's satchel, her rust coloured hair in modest braids.

He bought a book of raffle tickets to win the star prize – a double-bed American Quilt sewn as per usual by the women of the Baptist Prayer Group Sewing Circle.

He looked around for the Crowman and saw him prostrate, his hat all askew.

'It's the heat…'

'He gone done too much…'

'He ain't getting' no younger, I tell ye…'

'Douse him real good…'

Abe got propped up and immediately threw up over his suit front. The heat soon raised the smell of sourness.

'It's his heart.'

'It's one o'them strokes.'

'Get the Red Cross folk t'him.'

'Get the preacher, I say…'

Diverted from the hoop-la stall and the coconut shy, hoards converged to watch Abe Lincoln retch and vomit and be drenched in a cold-water cure. Kids with balls of pink floss rushed over from the sugar-candy bar calling, 'Come watch the Crowman dying.'

'I ain't beat by the heat at-all,' said the Crowman weakly. 'I been bit by a Black-Widder spider!' And he pointed to a wheelchair-bound grandmother with a tarantula looking thing crawling up her throat. 'I 'sturbed it when I was checking her sewed-up neck,' he spluttered and his eyes stood out like the spider's antenna. The ladies squealed and clutched their own throats. Someone scoffed,

'Old Martha Dukes ain't no lady-scarecrow, she gone died on us! No wonder I seen Denver Dukes speeding off a whiles back.'

Mostyn looked horrified and shocked in turn. He could hear his publisher saying with a smile: 'Deep'n'dark with little promise of a happy ending, Mostyn my boy. That's what we want!'

Abe was shook up real bad he told everyone. Real bad, even when the tarantula turned out to be a common Bold Jumper.

He eventually revived himself to pin a winner on the schoolgirl scarecrow's breast. Mostyn watched him stagger towards his road-battered pickup, saw it start-stop-start and race off like a devil-spirit was after it.

Twenty four hours later, Mostyn with a pink, blueberry and ruby-hued traditional American bed-quilt, was on the road again, another twisting back-track. Hills in the far distance. He wondered if he was heading for a dead-end. Still, he was in no hurry. By the increasing amount of scarecrow guarded fields, he realised he might be heading towards the Lincoln-Nance place. He came upon it, the buildings right up against each other. He couldn't tell the difference between the house and the rickety outhouses. He pulled up and decided to see how the Crowman was after his collapse. Fat pigs lolled about and scrawny hens rushed this way and that, picking and pecking like clockwork toys.

Mostyn knew Abe Lincoln-Nance was dead as soon as he saw the pigs snuffling around him and a chicken nestled in the small of his back. He dragged him out of the afternoon sunshine under the shade of an outhouse, covered him with feed sacks and a tarpaulin; weighed it down though the pigs had already started on his ears and the soft tissue of his cheeks.

72

Dipping with visiting buzzards, Mostyn saw telephone wires and followed them into the doorway of a kitchen of sorts to make the call. The sheriff told Mostyn thank you, and said he'd come out with the mortician just soon as he could... Oh, and would Mostyn stay until they got there. A hen clucked quietly from the top of a wooden dresser. Contents of an average larder took up all the surface space. Two cats eyed Mostyn from the comfort of Abe's grease-shiny pillow on a cot bed.

Mostyn moved into the outhouses, most of which contained what looked like leftovers from a disaster zone, stuff that remained after looters and scavengers had had their pick. Each section was as bad as the previous one until he moved into what he could see was the creation room. A gurney type trolley held a half-constructed scarecrow: straw and rags stuffed tight into sturdy legs of an industrial waterproof material. Mostyn looked closer; the work was pristine, stitches tight. This scarer-of-crows was to be a smart one, his feet and brogues had been firmly attached and a pair of tan-coloured cords was pulled up as far as his knees. His disembodied torso with poles protruding from arm holes and the neck was in the process of being sewn at the waistline with an upholstery needle the shape of a half-circle. The thread was strong and suitable for leatherwork. A yellow and green check work-shirt and a well-worn brown leather jacket hung ready on a dressmaker's dummy. The head sat like St John's on a platter. Mostyn lifted it carefully with two hands; it was perfectly weighted he thought, to balance and hold firm the hunter's hat decorated with green and gold feathers. Crucifixion crosses hung on bridle hangers around the room. Two were hung with complete dummies, both dressed in black as if for a dinner-dance: top-hat, shiny shoes, a cummerbund, and a matching red neckerchief to disguise the stitches. Four or five were in stages of half-undress. Two were lady scarecrows; one was a bride with a long veil that would blow in the wind and entangle the birds. In the next room, various and sundry clothes hung on hangers. Abraham Lincoln-Nance had taxidermy skills to be sure and was a perfectionist; Mostyn remembered the old joke about the crowman whose impeccable handy-work was 'outstanding in his field'.

He moved into the narrow passageway leading into what he could only describe as a family's 'best room'. It was set like a parlour. A bookcase full of encyclopaedias, a polished table, dried flowers in a vase. Rag-rugs on the floor, a standard lamp, a two-seater sofa, two easy chairs.

It took him a while to realise that the cushions on the chair, propped up a lady-scarecrow and the sofa too housed a lounging girl-effigy, looking at a Picture Weekly. They both had painted faces: rouge and lipstick and wide drawn eyes. Mostyn switched on the standard lamp and what he saw was a cosy, lived-in room, yet the utter silence told him there was no pulse of life in it. The woman on the chair was reading a book, her head cocked in concentration. On the sofa, the reclining girl's corn-coloured hair was like dried straw, her red plaid slacks and jacket seemed too big for her, as did her ankle boots. The three-stringed necklace was skew-whiff, and the pearls wore a dull sheen.

First published in *Cautiously Tiptoeing... Out of the Light* Sept 2020

There's More to Life than Death

I was a well-built house of fine proportions set in private woodland on the outskirts of a remote village. I belonged to monied landowners, the Hunters (and still do as far as I know), who kept themselves to themselves. Above my stone pillared doorway, my birth date is engraved *1850*, and I think I started to die in the year of 1960.

My unexpected rebirth happened sixty years later, quite by chance about a week ago.

It doesn't take long for a deserted property to look neglected. And when one has been neglected for long enough, one feels abandoned and derelict. I am not seen because I'm totally hidden within the private woodland of *Hunters Grange*. Surrounded by trees and large shrubs, I am to all intent and purpose, invisible. I was not intended to be discovered after my owners (who are extraordinarily wealthy, and able to make their own rules), ensured that nature took over to securely trap me as a spider traps its pray within the intricacies of her web.

Keep Out. Private Land. Trespassers Will Be Prosecuted. And to be on the safe side, a hand-painted skull & crossbones.

The area was sparsely populated in the '60s. After a few decades, older villagers ceased to wonder about me and the Hunters. Younger ones had other things to think about.

I never discovered why the family decided to disappear, but I felt it was something to do with the young daughter, Rosamund, who had been confined to the old attic nursery for months until she gave birth to twin babies. Girls. Within six weeks, *Hunters Grange* was wiped out by the family. They simply closed me up and let the grounds engulf me.

My dying was slow and lonely. First, I became blind when they shuttered up the windows from inside, then, silence told me I was deaf after they eventually nailed up the outside with sheets of corrugated iron. Mildew caused my lungs to hurt. Cold became colder. Isolation became absolute. Rising damp ensured my walls clung with parasitic green moisture. Dankness and gloom were my only companions. Decades came and went, and I existed as a stagnant heart and sorry soul.

The creeping, crawling ivy swallowed my body, Virginia Creeper forced its way through the stonework, smothering and suffocating me. I sank, weeping and sighing till I could breathe no more. Resigning myself to everlasting nothingness I finally accepted the living shroud, and gave up the ghost.

Unbelievably, last week I felt myself being born again. Something hovered about my closed eyes as a feather might, and pried them open. It was a weak light which had entered the room from behind one of the shutters. Watching it bravely crawling over the walls and floor of the sitting room was unbelievable to me; it was the first thing I'd seen moving since I'd died. I was mesmerized. Investigating, it was evident that the wooden shutter was falling apart and it took no time at all in easing it away from the window to see the iron sheets were also rotting away around the nails and bars. Through these jagged gaps, the light crept past the cobwebbed windows to overtake the room and for the first time in over half a century, I was reconnected to the outside world.

Starting to see again, my other senses returned slowly and worked together. I smelled decay and felt the nasty dampness clinging to my skin.

Before my eyes, there she was – a beautifully intricate living creature climbing up the walls – a black haired, lacy growth of fungus, her arms seductively hugging the dado rail, her nails clawing at it, and her limbs outstretched to reach the darkest corners over-riding the picture rails. She'd even thrown herself onto the bare floor, hands under the skirting board looking for company. She spread herself out, wanton and carefree. She wore skirts of mildew-coloured gauze: ash grey, pale lilac, cream. Shifting shape as she moved, she was living, yet gave off her perfume of decay and death.

My damaged lungs and ancient joints, scuppered my ability to move quickly, so Mildred (the name I gave to the beautiful creature) led me slowly from room to room, pointing her long, black finger-nails this way and that. She pointed me to the opportunists who'd moved in to the vacuum created by my death: living species had taken over, transforming their host into a magical new beginning. Wasps found soft wood to violate, make an entry and construct a most wonderful house, with layer after layer of fine craftsmanship, and in which, they had led a full living life. Each room held a botanical experience where mould and fungi had created a garden of unimaginable design and hue; bursts of outrageous colour growing and living on my corpse while I died.

I discovered life existing in every dank corner of my dead body. Looking at myself in the mirrors, silvered, fox-marked and cloudy, now reflect the change in me, of what I have become. Paintings were transformed as if the artists had magically appeared to use fly-blown smears and smudges to alter their subjects. Through boarded-up windows, sunshine forced its way in where the weather has taken its toll, and I saw dust-motes dance and shimmy in the warm rays before they land and create beds for prehistoric-looking woodlice. Flies trapped and dying, fed the spiders who work away at their webs, creating ever-changing stories.

A curious-minded robin, having sneaked through some tiny orifice, is now dead on the kitchen floor lying among other small bones, yet energetic arthropods investigate every feather and eye socket and beak, so that

77

it gives the impression that the bird is slowly moving, trying to find the way home. There is so much life in the long-dead me.

The privies have been living their lives too; the wooden doors had changed colour with every season. Sixty years ago, I remember the paint had already looked as if it was coming to the end of its life. Once, a bright red muted to a matt red. Matt red to a faded red, faded red to Rose madder, Rose madder to rust-red. Over the many winters and summers, frosts and blazing suns had peeled back the paint on the outhouse roofs to create a greeny-blue underpaint and I had missed witnessing its rebirth over and over to reveal today's mottled turquoise.

Inside the garden shed, the tools had taken on a life of their own on the rotting walls, hanging and clutching at each other like living people. The spades and shovels leaned in close to one another looking for signs of warm blood. Rakes' teeth smiled grotesquely showing their gaps of decay. Cornered banks of leaves turned into earth, and earth into a living compost of worms and bacteria. Rats scuttled.

Mildred led me upstairs: the attic Nursery door was closed. As I opened it, the loose floorboards caused the little rocking chair to perform a kind of slow dance, like children do when listening to nursery songs – *Hush little baby, don't say a word, Mama's gonna buy you a mockingbird...* and I then remembered young Rosamund. The room was furnished as I imagined it was when she was confined here. Oh, they hadn't boarded up this little window, it was slightly ajar and fresh air circulated. The cot was made up as if had been used only yesterday. I peeped in. Rosamund's mummified baby girls lay wrapped together.

There was no new life in this room.

The Evans Hotel, Llandudno

Ghosts abound whether we know it or not. You have no need to go looking – they'll find you. This story starts for me in the 1970s when my mother celebrated her sixtieth birthday. She was the kind of person who, when asked what she wanted as a present, would say, 'I don't really need anything', and we would start the game of – 'Oh you must want something, Mum!'

'No, no I'm quite happy, I have everything I need.'

And so it went on until eventually she gave in:

'Well, perhaps a night away in a nice hotel where I can be waited on. That would make a lovely change,' she said.

Great, we thought, we've cracked it. 'Who would you like to go with?'

'No-one.'

'What, on your own?'

'Yes. I'll be perfectly happy by myself; it'll be nice and peaceful.'

Our father had died only eighteen months previously and my sister Kay, and I were a bit concerned that she'd be OK. Anyway, we suggested a few places including Chester and The Grosvenor Hotel.

'Oh, no, I don't want to go far. Llandudno will be fine.'

'Llandudno! But that's only ten miles away!' But on reflection, I suppose Llandudno would make a nice change for her. It was after all, our largest town. So, Llandudno it was. And she didn't want to stay in The George, The Imperial, or The Grand, instead, chose *The Evans Hotel* on Charlton Street.

Of course, my sister and I asked why she should choose this particular hotel and how she knew about it anyway.

'It's all to do with the War,' she told us, and went on to say that during WWII she was recruited to work for the Inland Revenue in Llandudno after the department had moved various Revenue offices to this relatively safe area. Telling us there was a lot of camaraderie between them and that she actually had a sweetheart called Nicholas Murphy who did something in the Ministry of Defence. 'He was *very high-up* in the finance department, but, conspiratorially she added, 'all very hush-hush of course,' and she went on to talk about how during that time, everybody accepted that 'Careless Talk Costs Lives' and that 'Walls have Ears'. 'We understood it perfectly. We'd all signed the Official Secrets Act and we learned not to ask questions because the answer was always the same: 'Careless talk costs lives', so you see, we didn't question anything. That's the way it was in the War.' She was silent for a while, then: 'We grew very close, all of us, our small gang, especially Nicholas and I, but now I don't even know if that was his real name, sometimes he called himself Kivlechan – he and his friends were very elusive and mysterious. Perhaps that's why I liked him so much.'

My sister said, 'What about Dad?' and my Mum said, 'Oh that was a little while before I met your father.'

'But what has The Evans Hotel got to do with all that?'

'Well,' she said, 'I also worked some evenings for Mr Baker-Toole who managed the famous 'Catlin's Follies' at the Arcadia Theatre, and sometimes when things ran late, I stayed overnight.'

Then all three said together, 'at The Evans Hotel!'

I caught a glimpse of my mother in a different light. It may have been the way she looked at us, from one to the other, as if to say – I was young, once, too.

'What happened to the romance, Mum? What happened to Nicholas Murphy?'

'I don't rightly know,' she said quietly. 'As I said, that's the way it was. None of us knew anything really, not even when we'd see each other again. If ever.

Although her birthday was in July, she put off the visit to the Evans Hotel until a weekend in December 1971. She said she would enjoy the Christmas lights and then she said: 'Coincidently, December 1942 is the last time I ever saw Nick. He just disappeared… Where have thirty years, gone, hm?'

Not wanting to dwell too much on our mum getting nostalgic about someone she loved before our dad, we took our minds off Nicholas Murphy and concentrated on planning her birthday treat, booking her a nice room.

The weekend over, we collected her at about 4.30, just after they'd had afternoon tea; she was smiling brightly, too brightly.

'You have a good time, Mum?'

'Lovely,' she said, and I saw a small frown.

'What's up? What's happened?'

'Well, something really weird. I'll tell you when we get home.'

'No! Tell us now, Mum. We're not moving until you do.'

Looking around surreptitiously, she lowered her voice and her tone changed a bit, as if she wasn't sure of what she was saying. 'Well, it was last night.' She went on to say that she went to bed after a very nice meal with a group of guests, didn't read her book because the lamp was so dim, and soon settled to sleep. 'It must have been about 3am, and I woke because I sensed someone in the room. It was a man I know that. Because I could smell pipe tobacco – you know, when it's permeated their clothes? Quite a familiar smell I but I couldn't put my finger on it. And Brylcreem. A touch of Brylcreem! I've just remembered that.'

81

My sister and I looked at her, amazed.

'A man?'

'Yes.'

'And then what?'

Kay said, 'For goodness sake, Mum, what happened next?'

'Well, I was confused and pretty scared but thought I must have been dreaming. I made to switch on the bedside table lamp and as I put out my hand, I touched the roughness of tweed. I recognized it immediately. It was a tweed jacket.'

By now, Kay and I were a bit spooked, and must have looked it.

'You needn't think I was hallucinating; I can tell you it was real. Very, very real.'

'OK, OK, Mum – go on.'

'I… I had such a shock; I pulled my hand back. I could hardly breathe – then I felt the touch of a hand, a warm hand as if trying to find mine.'

None of us spoke. This was mad. And not like my mother at all.

'I started to pray,' she said. 'But then the man spoke, quite softly, and said, "Hello, Frances. Well, well, what d'you make of all this, eh? after such a long time?" The shock of hearing him speak made me quickly reach for the lamp and turn on the soft night-light. I saw him,' she said. 'I *felt* that I saw him and then I knew that I *knew* him.'

Her voice was just a whisper now. 'He seemed to move back, back towards the window, he doffed his trilby hat in a familiar way, and smiled. It was Nicholas.'

'Who?' we said together.

'It was Nicholas Murphy. I know it was.'

Now, my mother was a devout Roman Catholic and should not have been surprised to find a spirit of some kind

82

in her midst, especially a benevolent one who talked to her. But of course, she was surprised, but now, she said, not at all frightened. 'I was not *at all* frightened,' she said again. 'And then he was gone... but I could still smell the tobacco and his Brylcreem for quite a while after he'd left.

That my mother had entertained a strange man in her hotel room was something we teased her about for some time. That was over forty-five years ago; but recently the whole episode has begun to haunt me.

Researching a small project, I read about some secret wartime activity in Llandudno. Spies. The convoluted situation of counterintelligence involved secret agents, double-secret-agents and re-doubled agents. Double agents were often used to transmit disinformation or to identify other agents as part of counter-espionage operations.

This was like reading a Robert Harris spy-thriller in which, I readily admit, I end up not really knowing who is on whose side. The words 'Inland Revenue' jumped out at me from the research and I remembered that my mother worked for them. And when the 'Evans' Hotel' was also mentioned I read more carefully: apparently, at the start of WW11, plans were made, in the event of a German invasion, for German agents, now working for the British, to be hidden in hotels in North Wales. The Evans Hotel was one of these. The order was given that in this event (when the agents could easily swap sides – again!), they should be taken into the basement of the hotels and executed. This did not happen, and the plans were scrapped. But later, I read: 'while the war was still being fought, three of the spies, who it turned out were double- and re-doubled agents, proved to be so dangerous that they were indeed taken to the basement of the Evans' Hotel, and executed. I read out their names: John McArthur, Louis van Mercer. And Nicholas Kivlechan Murphy.

So, the man my mother had loved had betrayed his country – possibly both countries, I would never know.

In 1971 when he appeared to her, he knew my mother was unaware of his past, his secret, – and had the gall to come calling on her when she was vulnerable after losing our father.

One thing's for certain, while Nicholas Kivlechan Murphy may well have sat behind a desk at the MOD supposedly sorting out defence accounts, he was also conspiring to destroy ordinary people, including our mother, Frances.

(John Lawson Rae has written many books on Llandudno and I thank him for writing about the spies at The Evans Hotel. My mother did work for the Inland Revenue).

Commissioned by Dr DeAnn Bell and read at the Llandudno Festival of Light 'Ghost Story Event' December 2019. The story had to be based on a local, real event and take no more than 10 minutes to read.

Wait for Me

St Michael's Mount looks so near; you can just reach out and trace your fingers over the fairy-tale castle and slide them down onto the gardens and into the sea which is well-out now. Crocodiles walk across the causeway: families, kids, teenagers, old people, dogs. You sit on the balcony with a gin cocktail. You'd rather have a whisky chaser, but Joanie always liked cocktails on holiday. I know you miss Joanie, but still, life goes on, as you keep saying. Why didn't you ask for a whisky chaser, Tommy? Two, if you want.

You were eighteen and Lindsey was seventeen and you wanted to get married. Once you got home to Liverpool, your mother scoffed: 'It's only a holiday romance, f' God's sake, you'll get over it.' But in your letters, you said you wouldn't, and Lindsey said she wouldn't. Then Joanie came on the scene and that was that. Joanie even chose what tie went with what shirt and what newspaper you read, and you let her. Now, you've decided, it's going to be different.

The first thing you're going to do is move down to the sands and straight onto the causeway and stroll all the way over to the Mount. Take your time and try to find the same patterns in the sets; Lindsey found two fish, you found a footstep and a lop-sided tree. You might even recognize the rock pool where Lindsey slipped in, then had to take off her knickers because they were soaked and afterwards you said you couldn't help it, and she said, No, I know. That was the first time you'd touched a girl's privates and you thought it was like touching a sea-anemone. You want to taste that incredibly intoxicating feeling again, don't you? The ice cream hut and the little tiny shop that sold succulents and bags of shells? You might find the pearly shell that had a hole worn in it that you put on Lindsey's finger. You might even see Lindsey; she can't have changed that much. What will you do? Kiss her, touch her again? Oh, all the things you will do with Lindsey today if you should find the footstep and the lop-sided tree.

Tommy watches the castle become a silhouette, the tide edge its way in, and suddenly, rush over the cobbles with alarming speed.

Pretty Boy and Puggy

Pretty Boy really was pretty, and Puggy was, well, just Puggy.

They were our neighbours and lived with their Mom, Cindy, and sister, Suzette. Suzette was a coupla years older than the twins. When we came to live in one of the ticky-tacky shacks on the headland, the boys were about four. Everyone who lived on the headland had no place else to go. What I liked about it was, everybody looked out for each other. Cindy got a wait-on job at Smokeys so I used to mind the kids. We'd sit curled up on the huge old sofa and watch the brand new TV.

Pretty Boy laughed and played with his sister, singing and joining in the TV show. Most of the time, Puggy just looked bemused, and when he did respond, you could tell he didn't know why.

I pretended I was their Mom. We'd roll out pastry and make biscuits; Suzette and Pretty Boy ended up with stars and circles, but Puggy just kept rolling 'till there was only a grey stain left on the board. I liked looking after the kids; it meant I didn't have to go to school.

'How come you're called Pretty Boy?' I once asked. 'And, why Puggy?' Pretty Boy shook his head and coo-oed, 'I dunn-nno' and Puggy looked blank. Puggy hardly ever murmured but sometimes I saw into his pale eyes, they were drinking in everything around him as if he were real thirsty. 'Suzette,' I said, 'why do the boys have such names?' She put her little blond head on one side. 'We-ell, I think it's because Pretty Boy's so cute...' She opened her mouth to continue, then found nothing to say.

The headland was sorta picturesque, it rose up from a park of wrecked cars dumped near the pebble beach; on summer nights, the sun picked out all the shiny bits so the wave of wrecks sparkled like a fairy land. The shacks on the other side were just over the rise. The cliff edge wasn't far from our fence and the view over the top was breath-taking. Sometimes I couldn't speak for hours after I'd stood watching the sea. The horizon was a million miles away; one day I would get beyond that. The beach and the cars were our playground. The cars became whatever we wanted: carriages, stagecoaches, trains and wagon trains. Once the boys had ripped off the doors and re-arranged the seats, the cars, yanked three or four together, were soon transformed into a New York penthouse or a neat New England home. It was so airy and fresh up on the headland, it gave you a great feeling. The winter wasn't so good though.

Puggy was no bother at all; he was just there... nothing much affected him. The only time he came to life was when Cindy's mom came to visit. Gram-ma drifted in without warning and left the same way, like summer rain, always with a promise to keep Cindy posted. 'I'll keep ya'posted, honey,' she used to say through a cigarette each time she breezed out. Puggy loved her because she seemed on his wave-length. Every time she came, she had a different craze: she made tiny, knitted animals, shell-animals, crepe paper flowers, framed pictures outa coloured, silver paper, all sortsa things. She stayed a coupla days, a coupla weeks, whatever. Once she stayed for four months and Cindy went bananas complaining that this time, she'd got religion – 're-e-eal bad', an' all tied up with singing. 'She don't stop singing angel songs. All day long she's croonin' angel songs'.

'Sing-a-long-a Gram-ma,' Puggy was coaxed. 'Let's sing angel songs,' she'd say. 'They're so sweet, Puggy baby, so-o-o sweet and the sound goes wa-a-y up to heaven.'

Pretty Boy didn't need any second bidding; he was

good too, but it got so bad that Cindy went round complaining, 'Angel songs from first light! My home's taken over with angel songs.'

I'm glad I did so much with the kids 'cause now I've got a baby of my own; she's two months old and looks like a tiny Jodi Foster. I think she has the lips of her Daddy – I don't recall his face too well; I haven't seen him since my fifteenth birthday. I 'spect he moved on. I call my baby, Limpet, 'cause she sucks so hard… but I might change it to Jodi.

Gram-ma crooned a lot to the kids. She praised the Lord at every opportunity, blessed my baby no less than three times a week, got Suzette and the twins on their knees every night – and the angel songs! She never let up. 'Jesus can hear every word,' she told the wide eyed kids.

Suzette said, 'Every word?'

'Every single word,' answered Gram-ma. 'Up they go to heaven where the Lord listens and claps and begs for more. Heaven is a perfect, peaceful place, full of angels and beautiful angel songs.' She never let up – but she made me laugh.

'What the hell do my kids know about the Lord, what the hell does He know about them – we don't exist,' Cindy screamed at the end of her tether. 'Do-Not-Exist, Mother!'

Gram-ma liked the good feeling that went with singing – she meant no harm. 'We will gather at the river…' Pretty Boy and Suzette sang along happily over and above the TV. Puggy's little face only showed some light when they got to the chorus, '…We will gather at the river, the beautiful, the beautifu-ul ri-ver…' Boy, did it light up. Seemed like for once, Puggy's brain connected with words. Once, when the others were mucking in towards supper, I heard Puggy humming – and in tune!

Limpet also got Puggy's interest; I let him rock her when he was sitting safe between the cushions.

'River!' Puggy said one day like it was the most natural thing for a seven-year-old to say when he'd never ever spoken properly before. 'River!' Everyone screamed, 'Puggy said "River"!' We were all shouting and clapping, and Puggy laughed real wide. What a din there was in that shack, crying and laughing and whooping around, celebrating Puggy's first real word.

Gram-ma and her angel songs were getting through to Puggy. And for the first time in his life, Puggy became the centre of attention. Suzette and Pretty Boy showed off their brother; they were so proud. 'Puggy can ta-a-lk!' they ran round the site yelling, 'Puggy can understand!' But the novelty soon wore off when they saw how much notice was being poured on Puggy, and because Puggy only wanted to say certain words. He loved the sound of 'wewillgatherattheriver' and 'PraisetheLordinheaven' and 'SweetJesusmine', and 'LittlechildrencometoJesus'. He laughed and chuckled like a chicken for Gram-ma as she promised him a song if he spoke. 'Angelsong,' he chirruped happily. 'Sure, Puggy, baby, just so long as you say "Come-to-Jesus"'.

'River!' he said.

'There ain't no rivers around here to speak of, Puggy babe,' Gram-ma teased, not seeing Puggy's frown. 'No, sir, not round here, all you've got is a not too clean stream and the sea. You got plentya sea, Puggy, down the path there or over the cliff, you've got plentya sea! OK...' she went on like a train, '...so it's not cool and clear and bubbly and trickling over rocks, and there's no clutch of trees to shade under while you gather, but you can pretend, Puggy babe, that's how life is.' She was squatting down talking serious to Puggy's little screwed-up face. 'Come on, big guy, let's learn new angel songs.'

'River!' said Puggy.

The day Puggy nearly took Limpet away from me

forever, was the worst in my life that far; what followed just took the biscuit.

Y'see, for the first time in Puggy's short life, he was Number One, and Pretty Boy was pushed into the background. I don't think it was a good thing for either of them. Puggy was so used to being, well, just there. He was always comfortable with that.

'Gram-ma and her angel songs woulda driven anyone mad!' Cindy said afterwards.

Limpet was in her carriage, Puggy was half-heartedly pushing her up and down from where he stood. 'Angelsong, angelsong, angelsong,' he muttered as if he were in a trance. Suddenly he stopped and shouted at the top of his voice, 'I wanna be an angel! I wannabewithJeus-inaperfect-heaven.' We all shot up from the porch.

'IwannasingforsweetJesus…IwannagatherattheRIVER!'

Everyone looked astonished. No-one had ever heard Puggy say so much.

'There ain't no river, Puggy Babe.' Gram-ma was rigid with surprise. 'Only the sea, I told'ya honey.' Her voice floated like a feather. Puggy's voice got louder and he started to wail, 'I wannabewithJesusbytheriver. Iwannagowithhimtoheaven.'

'Come on in,' Cindy said, tight as catgut. 'Let's get you a drinka juice.' With that, Puggy snatched Limpet from her covers and ran towards the headland.

'There ain't no river…' Gram-ma whispered into the wind.

In a silence like I'd never heard before, the sound of two, big, white sea-birds squalling and screeching above Puggy, stopped him in his tracks. They circled tantalisingly way out of reach, swirling and dipping and calling. I don't know what made Puggy put Limpet on the ground; the shock hit us like a tidal wave and we all froze. Puggy, his little head raised up towards the white gulls, his arms out like wings, flew towards the edge like a bird. IwannagouptoJesusbytheriver!' And over he went.

The sea had never looked so pretty; it glittered and glinted through my tears, once I took my eyes away from Puggy's tiny body, caught like a chick in its nest on a bush near the bottom. All we could hear was the sea lapping at the rocks below us.

Puggy lay in a little white box ready for burial, his hair plastered neatly to cover the smashed skull at the back. He was decked in a white suit; I can't think where Cindy wouldn've got that. Gram-ma had embroidered angels on the white pillow and every time Suzette paid respects, she scattered petals all over him. Cindy and Gram-ma wept all day long and so did I. Pretty Boy did nothing; he was too stunned to speak. It was strange to see him looking so out of focus, in the background – all the attention poured on Puggy again. His face looked troubled like he was trying to make sense out of seeing his brother fly to Jesus.

Families came from all over the headland, made quite a day of it, bringing food and gifts for Cindy.

When they put the lid on Puggy, I saw his real name: Ira Schultz, twin brother of Lawson.

When it was time for Puggy to go, the Reverend Siseman came up in a car for Cindy and Gram-ma; they sat in the back with Puggy lying across their knees.

The weight of Puggy's death threatened to suffocate me, its strength and power so strong I couldn't wait for them to drive away and take with them the fear and terror I still felt when I thought about Limpet. I held her so close she almost choked. I promised myself I'd never let her know what nearly happened to her – what happened to Puggy; I promised myself I'd never ever think about it again.

The Reverend pulled away, the car crunching slowly over the cinder path. Just then, Pretty Boy let out such an anguished scream; he tore his hand away from Suzette and started to run after the car. Cindy's twisted face in the window mouthed, 'Go back, Pretty Boy, back to Suzette.' She looked so sad and beaten. Then her lips curled up and her face changed as if she couldn't believe what she was seeing, and I could see her, beating Reverend Siseman to stop. It all happened so quickly, although at the same time it was like in slow motion.

Pretty Boy, his legs gathering speed had vied off towards the headland; he was bellowing, 'I wanna be an angel like Puggy. I wanna be by the river, too.'

And as he flew over, not so gracefully as Puggy, we went through the whole thing, again.

First published in Infinity Junction's *Not for Bedtime* – chilling tales from around the world (2001)

Nothing Touched Her

It was 1995. November. The month that rattled her chesty cough and unsettled her mind.

'RymerDead! RymerDead!' Sylvie Lennon's cry was flat, clipped at the tail-end. She sunk her chin into her muffler but it wasn't the damp that caused the chill. Flat, delivered with a smoker's croak, she called into the slow, fine rain, her voice had as much emotion as if she were announcing a rise in the price of bread. That was Sylvie's way. Commuters off the 5.38 fanned out from the station archway and into the street. Faces in the yellow light indicated that some had already heard. No-one in the small town of Gortonshaw needed to ask, 'Who *is* Rymer?' No-one in the whole of Great Britain. The emotion kicked off by the very mention of her name never failed to ignite. It would not diminish with her death.

'RymerDead! RymerDead!' said the newsvendor into the evening air. She noticed a build-up of unwholesome interest ripple through the commuters. A relentless wave that had clung tight for three decades.

Sylvie trained to cry the news at her Gran's side. 'Evenin'News!' she called, her hands and curly red head showing from above counter level. 'Evenin' News!' imitating Lou Lennon and dipping into a little tin of coppers for change. She loved it down at the station pitch; the smell of steam-smoke air, the sounds of the trains hooting, 'swhoo-swhooo-swhoooo,' and the crowds spewing out of the archway, crowding round the stand, throwing out friendly chat to her gran. 'Ten Players, Lou, m'love, and my weekly…' 'Giz'a packet of Rizla and some mints, Mrs L… hello there, Sylvie sweetheart…' After her Gran's cry gave out, Sylvie took over the pitch and now she couldn't remember when she hadn't sold ciggies and mags, chocolates, mints and throw-away lighters to the city commuters, and calling out 'ScandalAsProfumoQuits!' in her throaty voice, and 'SpiesJailed'n'ThirdManNamed.' Proud as Punch, she delivered the news in the same excited voice as her gran's.

That was before 1965. Before Sylvie's mind shattered. Since then, her voice lost its enthusiasm, its animation. It was as dead as she felt. Today, she stated flatly, 'RymerDead! RymerDead!'

A middle-aged man spat, 'May she sizzle in hell.' He chose a bar of nut toffee with his paper. 'By Christ, may she sizzle…'

The old priest, in a black Crombie coat and felt hat, moved towards her from under the archway. Sylvie'd wondered when he would show up. He hadn't wasted any time.

'Ah, hello there Sylvia, my dear, how is the world wit'you?' Father Jerome shook his brolly and picked up some cough-sweets. 'Ah, 'tis the weather itself for the devil and his pals.' He perused the chocolate. 'Hah, this'll do nicely, y'remember I have a sweet tooth.'

'You've not been round here for months, Father.' She took his money avoiding his look but felt his eyes on her, scrutinising her face.

'No, no. No, indeed. It's just visiting I am. Looking up some old faces. Sure I'm not that far away, only in Brockleton Village and since I've retired, well, I have time on my hands so I do.'

Sylvie continued to serve her customers. One chose a nice glossy. 'Ta, love, one-forty-six, fifty-four change. Mind how y'go…' With her free hand Sylvie heaved a bundle of papers and sliced through the string with her knife, she layered them half-a-dozen thick, stacked the *Woman's Own*, replenished the Spearmint gum.

The priest tried again: 'I take it you're well in yourself, Sylvia?'

'Fair, Father, fair, considering the weather… and all this mist.'

'Yes, it takes its toll, so it does. Ah-mm, I was thinking I'd put you on my calling list today. Will y'have a cup of tea for me if I call on you this evening?'

'No. No, I don't think so Father… I may be out!'

'Ah-ha, well another time maybe. God willing.' He doffed his hat.

'Yes, Father, next time…'

Out of tune now, Sylvie sang: 'RymerDead! RymerDead!' She met no-one's eye.

The news reached the town where it had most impact, Gortonshaw. It spread quickly, people feeling they had a right to take it personally. Not Sylvie, though. News didn't touch her anymore. Nothing touched her.

Taxis and buses swallowed up the homeward bound and Sylvie took a short break.

Lydia Rymer. The infamous daughter of the city of Chestergate had died. Named the most notorious and reviled woman in the country after she and her lover had been found guilty of the murder of four little girls over a period of five years. Sylvie remembered shouting, 'AnotherChildMissing,' and the public saying, 'Let me get my hands on him,' and 'Hang the bastard by the balls.' And the incredulity when the murderers were identified! Two women: Lydia Rymer and Eva Quinn. Rymer and Quinn. The names rolled off the tongue as smoothly as Simon & Garfunkel, and Tom & Jerry. Quinn took her own life years ago. Despite that, their names were still inseparable: Rymer and Quinn.

The 6.06 arrived, whined to a halt. Sylvie served her

customers fluidly without looking at them: 'One-seventy-four – ta, love.' 'RymerDead,' she intoned as if she were telling about bad road conditions. The crowds momentarily wavered wanting to hear more. Gortonshaw folk felt they were entitled to more details but Sylvie Lennon never commented on the headlines, not even when her voice cried out: 'TragedyHitsHillsborough!' nor when she told the people: 'SchoolChildrenShotDead!' Sylvie knew all about the loss of a child, and talking about others was never on the cards.

'Sylvie's a cold fish,' commuters said. Heart of stone, they thought. No-one could get close to Sylvie. If they but knew, though. Tonight, Sylvie felt as if her insides were being liquidised. And now Father Jerome! 'I'd better buy a few biscuits,' Sylvie murmured, for yes, she remembered he had a sweet tooth, and knew he would call despite her trying to dissuade him.

It was 6.30pm. A customer said, 'Y'look worn-out, Sylvie. Tired.'

'I'm fine, Tommy, fine,' Sylvie answered but said to herself: I don't think I've ever felt wearier in my whole life. She didn't respond when he said, 'That's some news you're giving out tonight, Sylvie.'

Rymer and Quinn were public property. Their lives had been picked over by three generations of people. Rymer, only daughter of middle-class Gerald and Imelda Rymer, well-mannered, convent-school educated. Pretty face, fiery-coloured hair worn short and spiky like a halo when she was arrested in 1965. And Eva Quinn? A very young, thin lass from the slums of Glasgow. No one knew more than that. By taking her own life after twenty-three years in prison, Quinn was redeemed slightly by the public. At least she had some sort of conscience.

Older and more privileged, Rymer was the dominant

partner so everyone said. Sylvie heard her own toneless cry as if it were yesterday: 'RymerCorruptsYoungLover!' and then after months and months of Quinn's silence: 'LoyalQuinnProtectsRymer!' The pair didn't divulge how they met nor about their crimes. And never revealed where one of the children still lay: seven-year-old, Angela Marlow, missing since 1962. 'EvilPairKeepMum!' They left the child's parents in limbo. And that's where they'd now stay, it seemed.

The foggy air settled low, the streetlamps gave a mustard-yellow light through the shroud of drizzle. Was it Sylvie's imagination that voices were lowered, that couples walked closer together? Were there more flowers bought from Jadie's stall, did Jadie wrap them more carefully than usual? The heaviness in her chest moved up into her throat, she had to remind herself of the vow she made, that she'd never let *anything* ever touch her again. She lit a cigarette, buttoned up her coat and pushed her money-bag into the Nat West bank's night safe. That's right, nothing touched Sylvie.

Her flat was warm; she always left the fire on low. She took off her headscarf, shook out her hair, now a dull rust-colour, speckled with grey. She sat down and switched on the TV. There it was, the iconic, black-and-white mug-shot with the newsreader regurgitating the dark story of Lydia Rymer. Sylvie'd heard it all before of course.

'...Eva Quinn, Rymer's partner, committed suicide maintaining her silence as to the whereabouts of one of their victims...' 'Rymer's death earlier today is the final blow for Mrs and Mrs Marlow, whose child's body remains undiscovered. Sylvie watched the couple, their heads shaking slowly. Then Joe Marin, the retired detective who'd led the hunt for Angela, reiterated, 'The parents will never know closure.'

Sylvie closed her eyes against the pictures, her ears against the sounds. 'Closure', a new word. As if anyone concerned with this case would ever know closure. Sylvie kept her eyes closed. Saw a baby's face, birth-stunned and furious. 'A girl,' they said, 'you have a girl.' When they gave the child to her, a nun's caustic voice said, 'Six weeks, that's what you'll have with her, Sylvia. Six weeks and you'll be able to pick up the pieces and may God lead you into a useful life.' Another remarked, 'How did you get into this mess at your age. You should've known better.' Then Father Jerome, who'd just been ordained, tried a kind smile. 'Sylvia, my dear child,' he said. 'I've just the right home for your baby, a nice, comfortably-off couple; they're friends of old friends so I can vouch for them.' Sylvie remembered she could hardly speak for weeping, but she managed to say, 'But she'll disappear, Father. Will I never see her again?' and Father Jerome, sympathetic, 'If it's any consolation, she'll not go far. They're not many miles away. You know of course m'dear, I can't be telling you anymore. You just need to know it's for the best. And yes, you'll never see your baby again, but that's the way of the world in these circumstances, so it is.'

Sitting with her eyes still closed, she remembered Father Jerome who was a similar age to her, stroking the baby's downy red hair and smiling at the outraged look on the infant's face. 'See,' he said, 'she's got spirit and a mind of her own; I can see that even now. She'll be fine. She'll do well, I'm certain.' Bile rose in Sylvie's throat at the memory and she almost vomited as her time in the Home came back to her: the sickly smell of cheap, waxy soap and disinfectant by the bucketful, the metal laundry bins clanking their way between rows of sweating, heavy girls, fingers crimped like a slug's back. Empty cots. Without a chance to say goodbye and I'm sorry and I hope you'll be happy and… Oh, the cries of those girls! and her saying *she* wasn't going to cry when the time came. Her eyes shot open, she saw the TV as if through a heat-shimmer. Her tears were hot on her cheeks, yet she didn't wipe them away.

The TV voice: 'A spokesman said that Rymer's parents, now in their nineties, had no comment to make about their daughter's death.' Again, a young Rymer looked out at the Nation with her spiked hair and Sylvie saw the baby face with a rusty-red halo about her head and remembered the vow she made to keep track of the child. She'd told herself it should be simple, the towns hereabout are small and it'll be easy to find her. She recalled every word she whispered that last day through the tears against her baby's cheek: 'I promise you I won't interfere; I'll just watch from a distance. I'll never shame you, never let you know how your life began, never embarrass you. I promise,' and she'd let her mind wander to the future she'd planned. 'I'll trawl every clinic and school; with that hair you'll be easy to spot. I won't let on of course, never let on.' Sylvie didn't know if this was possible but she had to believe, had to have a dream. The dream kept her strong and it wasn't long before her dream became a reality. She couldn't believe how simple it *had* been to identify the child. She learned to be where she could see her without suspicion: in the prep-school playground, in the convent school concert hall. Over the years she even talked to Imelda Rymer: 'Yes,' Mrs Rymer told her, 'Lydia's got a position in the main library, the research department… and she's moving house again, buying this time, a small semi on Brookland Road.'

Sylvie pestered the council and eventually managed to get a flat overlooking the very house. She could look out of the window and see her daughter come and go, watch her leave for work, watch her return. Saw the girl she shared with. Setting up house together was all the rage, youngsters wanting independence, sharing expenses. Sylvie was content. It was an answer to her prayers. It was all she ever wanted, just to be near her daughter.

Today, in her flat, Sylvie went back to Friday, 12 November 1965, and she settled down at the window. There was a light on in the living room across the road and she wondered if Lydia was home yet, or was it her late night at the library? Sylvie saw nothing untoward. Nothing untoward until suddenly, she saw three police officers became seven, eight, more. She watched astounded as they made their way to the front door of her daughter's house. She heard one officer roar instructions, then they rammed the door. It was bedlam.

Lydia Rymer was arrested with Eva Quinn and Sylvie lost her daughter again. That's when Sylvie resolved never, ever, to let anything touch her again for as long as she lived.

Sylvie'd succeeded. Nothing *had* ever touched her in thirty, long, lonely years.

Now the TV cameras took Sylvie to a south of England hospice. It looked bleak. She imagined her daughter's body, alone in the morgue. She turned off the television, put the kettle on. Lit a cigarette.

Sylvie knew Father Jerome would call so she was not surprised when the doorbell rang. She put out another cup, the biscuits. He never failed to visit when a Rymer and Quinn headline hit the news desks.

'Hello, Father.'

'Hello Sylvia, m'dear. And how are you since I saw you earlier?'

'I'm fine, Father.'

'Ah-ha...'

They talked into the late hours. Father Jerome suspected she'd traced her child, seen her nearby even when he'd been visiting the Rymers. He said, 'I've never forgiven myself. I felt responsible so I did, for telling you she wouldn't be far away. I put the idea into your head, I know that. You'd never've been the wiser had I not tried to intervene. You'd *never* have had to go through this.'

'It's my fault, Father. I should never have taken advantage of you, but when you went to Uganda for all those years, I was tempted to see her, thinking you'd never know. But I'm all right, Father. I don't let anything get to me. Since 1965 I've been immune to everything. I feel I've been dead inside, thanks be to God.'

'And now?'

'Now?' Her eyes filled, her face twisted. 'Nothing's changed, Father! I'm fine.'

'Here, I've some tissues.' His voice was sad. 'I feel helpless, Sylvia. I have no words for you.' And he let her weep as if she would never stop.

Eventually: 'I lost her three times, Father, once as an infant, then when she… you know, went the devil's way, and now my child is dead and I feel such pity for her, Father! Is that so wrong that I feel pity for her after all she did?'

'No, Sylvia my dear. Not at all, not at all…'

'I hurt so much, Father. I can't stop the pain.'

'Ah-ha, there's a lot of pain.' He lowered his eyes. 'Indeed there is.'

First published in *Cautiously Tiptoeing… Out of the Light* Sept 2020

Backwater

Against a black tunic-top and pants and a black cloche hat pulled down over dark hair and mascara-bruised eyes, her white face looked lifeless. Having seen this look in a magazine, Febby Time cultivated it. The day she got that magazine, she decided she would get out of here and go someplace else. That glossy book of pictures was treasured along with a small make-up purse packed with pale powder in a box, a lipstick, tiny brushes and a little jar of face-cream, all retrieved after the blonde woman had fled. The woman had dropped her bag in fright when she ventured too near the scattered shacks and saw Boy-brother creeping around under the cinder-block leg stilts with his winkie-pecker bouncing about his dirty thighs; he was stalking a chicken, crooning and cooing baby-talk yet wielding a wood-axe ready to strike. Boy-brother had not seen many proper women so did not recognise her to be a well-dressed nosey-parker tourist with a husband in tow.

'Dear Lord!' the woman had screeched, her hand blocking her mouth.

'For fuck's sake,' her husband had shouted over his shoulder. 'You and your *wanting to get real near the natives* – for Christ's sake, let's get back to the boat.'

Febby'd frowned at the commotion and saw Boy-brother through the eyes of that woman. That's when she decided to get out of Vanity.

Southwest of where the Atchafalaya diverges from the Mississippi, the heat and waterscape renders the land lush and fruitful and in which all manner of life fights for survival. Febby walks on a familiar levee towards Vanity with miles of tranquil-looking swamp water to her left. Wild azalea hangs prettily from branches, host to honeybees seeking the sweet nectar and filling the air with its heavy scent. Water-hyacinths give the air a misty-blue look over the carpet-covering of duckweed. A cottonmouth snake glides over the aqua-carpet and makes for the shadows of Cyprus trees which appear to grow downwards under the weight of ghostly grey beards of Spanish Moss. Gnarled knees of Cyprus rise out of the water like grave markers in a burial ground. Febby sees it still and beautiful on the surface but doesn't think about the hyacinth's pestilential roots clogging the flow of freshwater, strangling and choking the life out of anything that requires light.

Ma came to meet her. 'Y're back child, what held yer?'

'Gram said I could stay, said now I was growing up, I needed my privacy. She said Gramps saw Janny down the town no better'n she should be. Down by the Two-Step-Stop Gas Station, Gram said.'

'Gram knows Janny's better off financial-wise down there than up here. Better off down there with Calendy and Aggi, they look after each other. Least they're not up here.'

Febby looked at her mother who did not look at Febby. 'You bring stuff?'

'Yeh. Bread. Cookies. Butter pack. Soap.'

Ma watched her pile the goods onto the table end. 'That's nice,' she said. 'I think I'll rest up awhile now you're back.'

Febby was the fourth child of Sukie and Carter Time, all girls. Boy came ten months after; then Sukie couldn't hold onto babies for more than a few months. When Boy was about four, twin girls arrived. 'A month apart,' Carter liked to say anytime somebody stopped to listen. 'According to this here calendar, Novie come just before midnight on the last day of November and her sister, Novie-Dee popped along twenty minutes later – how a-bout that!' Today, the Novies stumbled about feeding the pigs and hens, their eyes all but blind and Novie-Dee surely couldn't hear properly. The chickens stepped on tip-toe from under their clumsy feet. There was discordant music in the drone of insects, the squawks, the grunts, all played out in a suffocating wet heat.

'You aim to have any more babies, Ma?'

'Aim?'

'Yeh. Gram said you didn't have strength f'r anymore. Not after baby Winter.

'Aim? She don't know what she's talking 'bout! You none of you know and you, Febby Time, can quit reading them fancy books and fetch some fresh water! Boy! Boy!' she called in a thin voice, 'You come on in an' get scrubbed up. Febby, you go round up the Novies too!'

Having been dunked in the small tub fashioned by their father, Febby brought in the Novies. That's one thing he done right, Gramps had said when he saw the dammed-up pool at the edge of the stream, least Sukie can wash away the surface dirt. The tub always held moving water as it trickled in from a side stream which was fed by the slow'n'lazy bayou lying on three sides of Vanity. Today, Sukie struggled in with a plastic container full of fresh spring-water for drinking and she hoisted it up on the side by the sink above which was a mish-mash contraption of pipes and screws and strange bits of metal forming the means to draw water from the tub. It was always hit and miss whether or not it worked. Febby pinned down the Novies and pushed night-clothes over their heads all the while watching her Ma and thinking that Pa is a no-good apology for a husband and father.

'Carter!' called her mother. 'For God's sake pick up that baby and feed it some pulped biscuit. Can't you see I'm pre-occu-pied,' and Febby saw the lanky form of her father loping towards the box-cot and holding the infant up to the window light, gazing at it in wonder at what he'd created. His skinny face cracked into a toothless grin and he crooned. 'Just look at this bea-utiful girly-girl, what was made from me and my lady; just look how she's growed from that li'l dish-rag to a chunkyfatplumpyfat baby...'

Five-month old Winter Time had been born in the

105

coldest, meanest month that had ever been around and her mother was far from recovered after her eighth live-baby birth. This child already had the ability to ask with alert eyes where her next meal was coming from. Sukie's milk was still flowing, staining her vests.

'You're still in good working order, Sukie-girl,' Carter said, his hand moving on her backside, his eyes half closed and his mouth drooling. 'Yessir, and them paps are good'n'full and look real handsome yet.'

That night, Febby curled right up, arms around her legs with her knees under her clenched chin, heard her father pumping away at her mother and her mother crying as if she were hurt. Febby thought about her magazine and the learning books Gramps had given her. She would get herself out of here.

Spring water spat out of the rocks and Febby drew a kettleful. It dripped over her sneakers as she made her way to the shack. She turned on the gas bottle and stuck the kettle on a ring.

'Make a cup, eh, honey,' her mother said. 'Nice and strong…'

'That thing what Pa did to you last night. It ain't right, Ma.'

'What's that, Febby?'

'That doing; what he was doing last night. T'ain't right.'

'Ah, that…'

'Yes, Ma. That. I know all about it now and he just shouldn't be doing it not while you still hurt so much.' Her small voice, unused to speaking these words to anyone let alone her mother, faltered a little and before she knew it, the kettle started to hum and she lost the words.

'Now, don't you be worrying that dark head of yours, honey. Not yet, you don't need to think about them kinda things for a long time yet.'

106

'Ma, I am fourteen!'

'You still a child, Febby, still a child, and I don't want you to go much further with this, not in your saying, nor in your head. Your Pa and me, well—'

'Ma,' Febby frowned, 'you're not moving so good, you can't hardly get up'a that chair—'

'Oh, mind that boiling water, Feb, mind it good and let's have some a'that hot lemon.' And her mother lay back on the day cot and sipped her drink like she was a lady.

'What? You want to come stay down the town with us! What for, Febby, there ain't nothing for you here.'

'I want to find a job. I want to save money to get out of this place. Miles away out of Vanity. I want to work.'

Her sisters looked at her. 'Work! What kinda work?

'I'll do maiding, baby-caring, anything.'

'Down Town ain't like that! There's no *work* like that in Down Town. Folks is poor, real poor, Febby, they don't have money for maiding. Unless you can write like a secitary and do sums. OK, you'll never get a job in Down Town.' Febby knew fine well what job her sisters did. How could they turn up to Vanity with high heels and skin-fur coats, glossy handbags and treated hair unless they were selling themselves? Whores. That's what they were. And I will not stay to become a whore. I must find a way to get money enough for a bus or the railroad to get me away.

Swaying Winter on a hammock contraption, Febby watched butterflies and songbirds cloak the summersweet bush. Its scent clean and pure gave her a small feeling of hope as she pictured her future in another place. A turkey-hen gave a plaintive cry and in the long silence waited for a gobbler to answer. Rich in everything but money, Vanity provided them with fish and hare or some sort of feathered game on the table and her Ma conjured up a tasty stew with the onions, potatoes and roots her poaching-Pa filched. But if he'd had a mind to, Febby thought, he could have got them out of shacksville by saving the money he raised from stealing, instead of drinking and gambling at the Two-Fold Hut. Her Pa could have got them a chalet, windproof and dry, with a bed each and a place to…

'Febb-y!' Her mother's voice was not strong, but it broke her day-dream. 'Febby, girl, come help your Ma, honey.'

Febby knocked twice at the door. A nice house, painted the colour of last year's corn, curtains at the windows. A young worn-out-looking woman opened the door with a baby on her hip, another one wailed in the background.

'Ma'am, I'm looking for work.'

'Work.'

'Yes, ma'am. Baby caring, house chores…'

The young woman looked blank. 'I didn't advertise for anyone…'

'No ma'am. I'm just asking along the street.'

'The street?' she eased her head out and scanned the roadway. 'Is there anyone out there, anyone tell you to come here?'

'No ma'am. I'm calling on just about everyone in this street, see if they need help.'

From inside, the wailing increased and the woman looked at Febby as if she were not from the same world as she. She said, 'You better come on in.'

The nice house was a mess. Looked as if no-one had ever put a cloth to anything. Even Sukie made the shack look a bit cared for.

'I sure need help. Never thought to do anything about it though,' and she waved her free hand around the room.

'How many babies you got?'

'Two.'

'Just two?'

'You sound like you don't think that's enough.'

'That's enough ma'am.' Febby took in the junk, the dirty clothes, the kitchen piled high with dishes and half-used cans of food. Three cats sunning themselves on the window ledge.

Cats! thought Febby. And this woman can't even look after two babies! 'You got cats?'

'They keep coming in – seem to like it here. Strays, I think, won't let you touch them, just seem to like coming in, feeding, sleeping around.'

Febby had never seen such a state. Not even when her mother was at her lowest and hugest with another child. Of course, Febby had to admit, their shack had hardly anything in it to get messed up. 'You want me to start doing something?'

The woman looked at her, nodded, sat down and suckled the baby. Slumped with her tight face screwed up like Febby had never seen, she cried silently, her mouth drooling.

Febby knew that Jay Backshiel lived in this house. Jay Backshiel of Jay's Cabs, Jay's Launderette, the One-Stop Gas Station. The Two-Fold Hut. Backshiel also owned some run-down apartments backing the launderette. Backshiel would have been real wealthy in a more prosperous town, but here, there wasn't money for fancy stuff, just money to get by. Some of the men-folk, though, they seemed to have money for anything they wanted.

Eventually: 'Mrs Backshiel, ma'am, my name's Febby Time and I live in Vanity. I aim to work my way out of there and so I am at your service, ma'am. Any time of day or night, I will do anything to earn some money.'

The woman nodded. 'I'm Ruby. Ruby Backshiel.' She didn't look anything like a ruby, more like a pearl: grey-pale face with a silvery sheen to it, oyster coloured hair, unclean. Even sitting she appeared to droop.

Febby didn't make much headway. She stacked five

sacks of garbage, pure no-nonsense garbage, out by the bins and the place didn't look any the better for it. And she watched as the woman slept with abandon on the sofa. Two infants, one still latched loose-mouthed to her, dozed too. Taking in their flushed faces, shallow breathing and half-opened eyes, it appeared to her as if their sleep was not natural, as if they'd had too much medication.

Two hours later, Febby put down a mug of ice-tea on a small table she'd cleared. The babies still slept. Ruby Backshiel whispered thank you between dry lips and seemed unable to reach for the tea. Febby unwound the baby from her arms and tucked it next to the other child. Two little girls. 'Here,' she said, 'sit up a bit and drink this. I have to go soon.'

'Go? You can't go now, you've just come.'

'I… I've got to go. Mr Backshiel'll be home soon…'

'No. He doesn't come home too much.'

'Why?'

Ruby closed her eyes slowly. 'He's real busy…'

'Ah-ah—'

The baby moved and her mother put out an arm to still her. 'Looks like you came at about the right time. I was about hoping there wouldn't be too much more of this.' She looked at the children and then towards an opened bottle of cough syrup, honey coloured.

'Ma'am, I will come back tomorrow. I can't stay right now.'

Ruby nodded. 'You will?'

'Yeh. Can I get a neighbour? Surely a neighbour would come in till I get back. You have good neighbours here, surely, you have?'

'No. Please, no. I can't have that.'

'There must be someone.'

Ruby shook her head from side to side. 'No.'

'You have a doctor, Ruby? I'll get the doctor.'

'No. Jay says the doctor'll take the babies. I've had trouble before…'

Oh, my – what to do next? Febby knelt down then backed away from the smell of unwashed skin. She took hold of the woman's hand. 'Ruby, I don't know you but I see you need some kinda help. I promise I'll come back, but I must ask about money. I can't work for nothing. I must have money.'

'I have money. That's no problem. If you promise not to call a doctor, promise not to call Jay or anyone else and promise to come back, I'll pay you real, real well. Go open that drawer, that one under the desk. You'll see.' Sure enough there was more money than Febby had ever seen in her life. What was this woman doing in such a state of chaos with so much ready cash? Money being the answer to all Febby's needs, she could not fathom out why Ruby Backshiel was in such a mess.

'Can I take money for a ride home and means of getting back? I need that or it'll take too long.'

'Sure. I don't know why, but I trust you.' Ruby Backshiel had no other choice.

Remnants of a failed catfish-farm enterprise, the shacks of Vanity were made up of washed-up timber, corrugated tin, match-wood and tarpaulin. Built on a dirt track two miles away from the clam-shell road and enough distance from the main highway for people to forget it existed.

Febby walked into the shack. Ma was up against the sink, retching bile and blood.

'Ma!'

The Novies crept in and Boy sidled up too and they stood watching, all agog.

'Ma, y'don't look good.'

'Never mind me, how you doing?'

Febby told her mother about the mess Ruby Backshiel was in, and her mother could not understand it.

'A proper house... plush seating places, kitchen things and money for un-necess-aries... and she's in a mess?'

'She is Ma, and drugging the babies so they don't make no bother...'

Ma's eyes went slowly from the Novies to Boy – all three, simpletons, then to Winter's box-cradle and to Febby.

'Ma, I may have a part-time answer. Just till you're sick no more.'

'I ain't sick, child. Just tired out what with everything's been goin'on. Everything's just caught up with me and I ain't young like I use't'be. I don't cope like I use'ta... not no more.'

'Shoo out,' said Febby to the kids. 'Me and Ma's goin'a talk some.'

'Sure. Light up the kettle Feb, there's a good girl.'

Febby buttered crust fingers and called out to the Novies and Boy as if they were stray kits. Lemon tea and cookies for Ma.

'You thought this all out don't'ya?'

'Yes, Ma. It's an answer, ain't it?'

'It's an answer, child.'

'But not a word to Pa, Ma. Not one word.'

'You might cut my tongue out first,' said Sukie.

This was it! A way out of Vanity. 'It's a good money boost for you, Ma.'

'I never took no charity.'

'This ain't charity, it's work. I can do this for as long as it takes for me to get out.'

Febby saw Sukie's eyes widen.

'What's the matter, Ma? I said something?'

'You're saying you're aiming to leave? When you've earned enough, you're gone—?'

112

Febby's mouth twisted up when she saw her mother's face.

'Aw, ma, don't do this. You said it was what you wanted. Me gone from here and not go the same way as the others—'

'I did. I did, child. I did.'

'It'll take a good while, Ma. I'll be here some time yet.'

In the undergrowth, crickets sang.

Febby noticed this better way of life gave Ma a new-found sense of worth, some confidence so that when she said No she sometimes meant it. When she put her foot down, it sometimes stayed that way and her Pa didn't know how to handle it and being a lazy no-good son of a bitch, didn't fight too long. For three weeks he'd been shacked up with a lady friend called Lupin. Lupin Yates, who'd spied Carter when he was jobbing for a Mister Lafayette down by the soybean field. 'I live up yonder. You a fine looking man,' she'd said in a sing-song voice, and though Carter knew he wasn't, saw his chance. 'I'll be right over, just's soon's I finished here...' She, a half-wit by anyone's standard, might have been a wealthy princess from a story book; he a prince, he took her hand and she led him into her palace. The trailer was almost the size of the Carter shack but, devoid of kids, seemed spacious, and he settled in without a thought for Sukie. Lupin Yates was also a religious maniac and filled Carter's brain with half-quotes to suit herself and make him side with her against whatever small amount of better judgement he had.

A kind of peace lay over the Time place. Sukie smiled and said how she liked the bed to herself. Life was better without Carter.

Cicadas and swamp frogs talked and chirruped into the warm night and rain dripped steadily, pattering and shifting the clamshells. Sitting on the porch, Febby counted her money. But how could she leave Ma and her siblings? Febby convinced herself that Ruby was improving, and that Ma would be OK if she could get money to her. A mink screamed the sound of a human cry which echoed across the creek, and hopelessness hit her as she realised that Pa had to come back if she was to go.

'Pa. You need to come home for Christmas. They're all missing you.' Febby was uncomfortable; she knew she was inviting him back to start messing with her mother again. 'I have plans, Pa. I'm going to make something of myself. Send money home to you.'

'Plans?'

'Yeah. I'll send money.'

'Y'are? Y'sure?'

'But you got to do better than you have been doing…'

'Mouth, girl. You watch your mouth to y'ol Pa.'

Febby narrowed her eyes, and gave him a mean look.

'I'll send what I can, Pa, but you must pull y'weight. And leave Ma alone. She can't have any more babies.' Mosquitos buzzed in the heat, and she watched his sly face.

'You growing up nice,' he said, and ran his finger down her front.

'You dare, Pa! You dare—'

'I dare what I like in my own home. You need to stay, Febby Time. It's your place what with your Ma so sick.'

'Ma's not so sick. She's better, getting stronger.'

'You keep on at the Backshiel place, keep bringing that good money in and we'll do just dandy.'

'We? What? You're coming back, just like that?'

'I guess.'

'Why? Why you coming home so easy?'

'Lupin done throw me out. Said I was a heathen.'

Febby stared at the place she kept her money.

Horrified: 'Pa, you been in my room?'

'No,' he lied.

'Where's my money?'

'That's family money. Fam-il-y.'

'No, Pa...'

'Oh, yes. You got to learn we share in this family. Share,' he said sidling up to her, pinning her against him.

He'd never done this kind of thing before. 'You lay off me, Pa. Ma, help him off me!'

But Pa was powerful. Screaming, she went for his face.

Pa whined: 'Ma can't help you, Feb, not no more. She's done for.'

'No. She's fine.'

'You blind, girl? Blind to what's clear to them who can see?'

'She's doing fine,' she kept pummelling him, losing strength.

'Bleeding from her front and back. You call that fine?' You call that fine when her cot sheets are soaked and her chest is cove in? She won't see Christmas...'

'She will so.'

His lips moved over her face and neck. She felt him grind against her, his breathing course and ugly.

Cringing, she half-choked, 'Pa... don't.'

Afterwards, Febby stared out over the wetlands. The moon's pearly face bobbed about on the surface, dismembered by the backwater disturbance.

———————

First published in *Cautiously Tiptoeing... Out of the Light* Sept 2020

Dead End

Ants crawled from under the bed like traffic, along the carpet, round the wash basket, up and over the bookcase with unrelenting determination. Lucy sat back on her heels, her face furious; she breathed heavily and started counting back from Ten. It didn't work.

'The Queen is lost, they won't survive without her.' Her face was white and anguished. 'Find her find her find her find her!'

Oh, no, not again. 'You were playing so nicely for a while, my lovely. What's the matter now?' I knew I'd get no sense out of her, just an ugly scream. I gave up. I was getting nowhere with this new approach. I was told there is no 'one way' to deal with it. Tell me about it, I'd thought. I'd gone down every avenue I was directed: ignoring, disciplining, humouring, explaining, distracting; responding with kindness and understanding, even though I wanted to throttle her. 'Shall I help you to find her, darling?'

She gave me a look of disgust: 'I told you she's fucking lost, you idiot.' Spittle foamed down her chin; her eyes dry and full of hate. 'Don't you know *anything*?' She swept the cardboard ants into a pile and pounded them with her fist. I left.

I couldn't see a glimmer of hope as we took one step forward and three back. I was at the end of my tether which was pulled so tight, I could have slit myself free of it. And her.

I thought about last year's acute obsession. Snakes. Lucy knew everything there was to know about snakes and said: 'Mum, can you get a scientist to come here and change my genes to that of a snake?' Her vocabulary and diction were precise for a ten-year old. When I tried to explain that that was absolutely impossible, she smashed her head open on the garden wall and I faced more questions at the hospital.

I tapped at her door.

'Shall I draw another queen for you, hun?'

No answer.

'Just until she returns?'

Her head bent low, she sang softly as she gently steered the ants back into their line, heading straight for the nest she'd made for them.

Lucy and the ants knew exactly which road they were taking.

The Molly Boys

The days alternated between unseasonable warmth and cold spells, Quinn found the road and hills pleasant to walk, though the evenings had him wondering about the winter nights to come.

The village had one corner shop and there in the window he read of a football match between the Yellow Boys and the first team from Minffordd. Teas served afterwards. The Massed Silver Band Competition was on Sunday. Two black edged cards announced with deep regret that Evelina Primrose Jones of 2 Riverside Cottages had passed away in hospital after a long illness, bravely borne, leaving her dear husband Mallard Easter Jones; and that William Williams of Broad Street had died suddenly at his daughter's home in Maentwrog. He looked at the cards for a long time and saw things for sale and wanted. He saw that there were a few odd jobs and he made a note or two. His chest was painful and with every breath it stung bitterly within his rib cage, raw and as if it were open to the elements: red and bleeding and closing in. He could feel thick and heavy mucus blocking his airways each time he inhaled. It was five o'clock and getting dark very quickly and by and by lights came on in the houses and in the *Queen Alexandra's Public House.*

He made for the pub about 7pm and therein, took a seat, ordered a whisky chaser and a plate of chips. The landlady brought it on a tray for him with extra bread and butter and a large bottle of tomato sauce: Here, she said, get this hot tea down you too, and surprised, he thanked her. He was surprised by an influx of men, young and old, freshly washed faces but still in their work clothes and all carrying musical instruments in black cases. Even though he understood nothing of the language he could tell that although the chat

118

was of little significance, it was tinged with excitement. The landlady told Quinn they'd been to the Young Men's Institute to practice for the Massed Band Competition, that it was a contest on home ground and to win that would be a big boost, but of course that wasn't the end of it – No, they'd be competing in Bala and Llandudno and in a little place just outside Pwllheli leading up to Christmas time when all the local bands and choirs got together for a carol concert and that caused problems too, with men able to sing as well as they could play, and where would their loyalties lie? Yes, problems every year with that one...

Silver?

Yes, Silver Band. Well, silver plated...

Of course.

They're all brass really but ours are coated in a thin layer of silver and what a difference! The sound's mellow, smooth as cream. Some instruments are nickel plated or lacquered, but it's Silver for us. You should hear the sound when bands get together! She slapped packets of crisps and scratchings on the bar, and went on: Twenty-five musicians plus percussionists and a conductor in each band and when they mass, well, you should just hear them – talk about goose pimples! Heart of the community the bands are. Spirit of the place I can tell you. Yes? What can I get you, Alun? Modest half-pints all round and without seeming to, the men took up their positions and treated the customers to a sweet rendering of *Ar Hyd y Nos*.

Next evening, Quinn made for the Queen's Public House again and didn't mind admitting that he felt a great comfort there; he took up the same seat on an old settle and partook of the same meal and just after eight o'clock, in came the same men carrying the same cases and this time, Quinn was included in some of their chat: You'll come to the Institute, Sunday?

119

Sunday?

Yes, afternoon. Big do. Annual it is. Helluva big do for us! We play for the quarry. Quarry Silver Band we are.

Roland Morlais Jones and his brother, Edward Morlais Jones introduced themselves. I'm Rol Molly and this is Ted Molly, and they went on to put a pint in for Quinn. Payday! said Ted Molly and he jingled a pocket full of coins. Quinn bought a small round in return and soon they had drunk four whisky chasers each.

What y'doing round here?

Travelling?

Travelling, eh? Funny place to stop, Bethesda.

Well, I'm not travelling in a travelling sense of the word...

But you've come over the water with a twang like that!

Yes indeed, yes I have. But I'm nearly local, I've been around for some time, so I have, you know, all over really, working here and there.

Oh, aye?

Yes, always on the lookout for a job.

We got a job for you.

Have we? One brother to the other.

Yeh. All Mam's stuff.

Christ, Rol, y'can't do that!

No. Neither of us can so we'll get Quinn here to do it. He'll be respectful, won't you?

I'm sorry... what do you want of me?

Mam's stuff. Needs clearing out. Disposing of. She died in August. August before last, said Rol, so it's time it all went whatever you say, Ted.

I... I'll do anything to help, but...

The brothers discussed this new development, this unexpected opportunity to do something about their mother's possessions, and Rol Molly said, I don't know how we hit on you, why you seem to be just the man to do it… there's something about you that says you'll be ok with the job.

Quinn looked surprised: But surely… surely you have someone closer, family to do such a thing…

No.

It'll be fine, said Rol. Fine. We can all chip in. Get it over and done with. And his brother nodded his head. Ok, I'll go with you. Final decision, Rol. Final.

Thinking about the remainder of his money, Quinn said No to the next round but he was ignored and more drinks flowed.

We're y'staying?

Oh, here and there…

Homeless y'mean?

Not quite.

Y'don't look very well, if y'don't mind me saying. Flushed and that…

Ah, it's a chest infection I have. Comes and goes you know how it is…

Come home with us tonight, plenty of space at ours, early start tomorrow on Mam's room, then final rehearsal before the big day.

But the clearing of Mam's room didn't start until February.

The Molly brothers lived at Menai View, a detached granite and slate built house which stood two miles above Sling and looked over the undulating landscape towards the Irish Sea and the straights. It had once been a fine small holding with animals and out-buildings to house them; now those buildings were full of junk and not even a pet dog to be seen.

Used t'be buzzing with work when Dad was alive but we were too young to carry on and Mam lost heart, got rid of everything she did when we got the insurance and then dad's brother, Uncle Morlais came to live with us and the money rolled in from his factory in Bangor. Made Bakerlite things he did: clock cases, picture frames, brush and comb sets, flasks, radio cases, telephones – all colours; napkin rings and fruit bowls. You name it, he made it!

Bakelite. There was so much of it about the house; Quinn remembered his Aunt Maura's dressing-table set, a mottled-green-backed hand mirror and he putting it to his nose to take in the scent of it and her.

We had pots of money then, didn't we?

Yeh, pots. Still not too badly off today, even though Uncle Molly died a while back. Left us comfortable. That's what mam always said, left us comfortable.

Bundles of newspapers and magazines lined the narrow hallway and they had to walk in sideways from the front door, tilting and staggering under bags of chopping-up sticks and shopping. Most of the rooms smelled of the boys' mam; a sweet sickly scent of stale clothes and strong perfume as if it was still regularly dabbed about the place. The furniture was steeped in the same warm spicy smell as he sat down and the kitchen smelled of cold bacon fat, fried eggs and fish. Empty beer bottles piled into a milk crate by the back door, and pilchard tins dripped their golden juice onto the quarry-tiled floor.

Quinn, happily ensconced, wallowed in the comfort of this time-stood-still house; he did his bit by cleaning the place after a fashion and sorting out the yard. He got used to a dark blue van pulling up and the two brothers buying an incongruous assortment of goods from the back of this mini-shop: matches, a torch, sweets, cellophaned sweaters, pairs of trousers, socks, Donkey jackets, a Davey Crocket hat and a bobble-hat, candles, tablecloth, tea towels, underpants and firelighters…

That first Sunday morning the Molly brothers said it was chapel for them: It wouldn't do not to go today, they said, All the band goes today, and so Quinn went too and understood not one word, but bowed his head when everyone else did and wore an interested look on his face as the minister spoke in a funereal voice.

No booze till after the concert, Quinn, not today. So the unlikely trio sat primly in the back kitchen of Menai View with ham and tongue and mustard doorsteps, mugs of tea and half a dozen fancies from Spiers' for their early lunch. The brothers speculated who they'd see today, who would play for which organisation, who'd choose chapel over quarry and vice versa. They said they hoped to see old Tommy Twice and explained to Quinn that Thomas Thomas had been known by this as long as they could remember, and then Ted said to his brother: Tell him about Bobbie Three-Times, go on Rol, and for a while they couldn't stop chuckling and Rol said, I don't know why we still laugh at that, it goes back yonks ago, to when Bobbie's family came here from Llandegai, his dad was a quarry manager and on his first day in school he was asked to tell us his name. No one knew he had a bad stutter, and he said, B… B… B…obbie-Bobbie-Bobbie and the whole class cracked off laughing and we lads got the cane and the girls got detention… Now, over thirty years later, these three were doubled over laughing and Rol choked on his tea and it spluttered out of his nose onto the floor and Ted swiped him with a tea towel and called him a dirty pig…

Quinn took a seat at the back of the Institute room and tried not to think about Tommy Twice and Bobbie Three-

123

Times, because when he did, he had to feign a coughing fit and stuff his handkerchief into his mouth.

Swags of crepe paper trimmings hugged the walls and his head brushed them; paper chains hung from corner to corner and from corner to ceiling light and big paper bells hung low with the weight and he watched someone trying to tie them up out of the way. The large room was packed and soon, the scent of many people filled the place and the place buzzed with talk. The stage was set with a huge Christmas tree festooned with trimmings made from silver, red, green and gold milk bottle tops glinting and winking in the lights of a darkening afternoon. Three judges sat facing the stage with papers and jugs of water. There were five competing bands, a junior band, the school-children's choir, a male and mixed voice choir and the competition went on until seven o'clock with a hand-bell-ringing interval at 4.30 for more sandwiches, cakes and barabrith served on china tea plates. Quinn slept on and off in the warmth and to the sound of little children and rich mixed voices. The Quarry Band came second. A post mortem was conducted in the *Queen's* afterwards and by chucking-out time most men were drunk with the headiness of it all.

And so Quinn settled for a while in the home of the Molly boys and by and by they took Quinn under their wing for Christmas. They said they would like his company because it wasn't the same at Menai View with only the two of them round the table; Quinn wondered at the developing familiarity, how readily and easily he slotted in, found himself surprisingly, quite at home for now. So Christmas in 1963 came and went in an unaccustomed combination of alcohol, and sex in the vicinity. The Molly boys said it was a Christmas present to each other. Prozie-

Presents they called it. We don't bother much after, they said by way of explaining the women who came to Menai View and lolled all over the place smoking endless cigarettes and drinking brandy and Babycham and cherry brandy and apricot brandy. Someone called Melinda-May had spent most of last Christmas here too. Best Christmas I'd had in ages, she told Quinn. She cackled as she fanned out some one-pound notes and waved them under his nose: Might as well come here as be on my own. She and a younger woman, Beryl, stayed for Christmas dinner and were in no hurry to leave and for all he knew it, stayed all night. Quinn thought there had been three of them but they seemed to blur and blend into each other and he thought he might have been tempted by one of them, and all this in a fog of pop music and pep-pills. The Molly brothers seemed to have plenty of money at their fingertips and bought presents for anyone who might call; piled on the parlour table were fancy soaps and novelty soaps, embroidered handkerchiefs, shaving cream and gift boxes of Old Spice, nets of golden chocolate pennies, and boxed frosted fruits, bottles of sweet sherry and Gold Label beer, tangerines and nuts and fountain pens with spare nibs. They even had a portable record player – an up-to-date Dansette that held several records at once and played them in order. They said they'd hoped to buy a goggle-box as a special treat but the television reception was not too good hereabouts, so they'd wait. The boys knew a lot about music, they took it in turns to play their favourite records, Ted Molly liked the crooners: Pat Boone, and Perry Como singing *Catch a Falling Star*... he loved Connie Francis and sat dreamy-eyed as she sang *Fallin', Fallin' for You-o-o da-da-da-a*... and Ray Charles in his creamy-gruff voice singing *I Can't Get Over You*... Ted spent ages trying to choose which song he'd like as his 'last waltz' in

125

the Winter Gardens with his dream girl. Rol Molly was into pop singers and rock'n'roll: Bill Haley and His Comets, Bo Diddley and Richie Vallens. Quinn was quite taken with his choice of *Bird Dog,* by the Everly Brothers; the late, Buddy Holly Greats, and Jane Morgan's *The Day The Rains Came Down...* and he liked Johnny Cash and Joan Baez and Bob Dylan who were trying to tell him something deep about the future, and Laurie London's *He's Got The Whole World in His Hands,* who was leaving it all to the divine mercy of God. Quinn had noticed that except for newspapers and music magazines, there was no reading matter in the house, but for Christmas, Rol had bought a copy of *Lady Chatterley's Lover* and joked that he had it wrapped in brown paper to keep it clean; he wouldn't divulge from where he had acquired this tantalising book, tapping the side of his nose and saying That's for me to know and you to guess, and his brother thumping him, trying to guess and saying, Go on, tell... The pile of gifts diminished by the day.

The women seemed not to leave at all over the holiday but they must have done and Quinn felt shame that he should have gone along with it all as if this was the usual way of things.

He'd had an eventful year, he thought. Eventful because of all the people he'd met and got involved with. It had not happened quite so fluidly before. Never in all the years he'd been wandering did he ever get too close to anyone for fear that they might find a chink and intrude on his secret... but now... his mind went over the soft women he'd got close to, Alys Mostyn and Bella Nanney, the people he thought of as friends – Ryders and Kits Nance, the Trilby'd Man; the Molly Brothers... Yes, he'd got close to these folk and he didn't think it felt too bad. He couldn't get beyond the

126

thought of Bella Nanney he realised, without feeling the sense of a small loss. He wondered what 1964 might bring.

Quinn's health took a turn for the worse and he was holed up in Menai View for three weeks without doing much except bark up dark green phlegm onto sheets of newspaper. Ted Molly took it all downstairs and put it on the back of the fire: It's nice having someone to look after, he said. I'll get some lemons and make a hot toddy and get the doctor to that chest of yours, and he did that and towards the beginning of February, Quinn was restored a bit.

Eventually, it came to Mam's room, a room of stagnant calm but in contrast to the rest of the house, with not a thing out of place.

The Mollys had decided: we'll give some to the Sally Army and some to the church jumble; there's not much for the bin 'cause Mam had good taste.

Mrs Letty Jones' wardrobe and chest of drawers stood against honeysuckle and sprigs of spring flowers embossed on good wallpaper. A square of flowered carpet took centre stage and a bedroom chair still with a spare embroidered quilt over the back. Quinn packed floral bedding and towels and put aside a velvet-trimmed jacket and a swagger coat with big black buttons right up to the neck; winter coats and suits with matching hats. Shoes and bootees. The boxes neatly stacked ready to be taken down stairs and Ted Molly nervously hovering. The boys' mother had been a tidy woman and there wasn't much to all this clearing out. It was just that her boys were reluctant to dispose of their mother for that is how it seemed to them. Quinn got Ted Molly to start taking down the boxes then set about the four suitcases chock full with more of her things. Three of them, tan coloured canvas affairs, each neatly layered with clothes;

the first, full of summer blouses, jumpers and cardigans, all folded in a precise manner and placed in colours of violet, pale green, and sky blue. The second and third case held winter skirts of tartan and tweed, woollen twin-sets, scarves, mittens and sheepskin gloves. As soon as Quinn opened the fourth, a rather smart, red leather suitcase, he smelled the perfume, the same strong, spicy perfume which hung about the front parlour. *Musk L'Amour* it was called. A big bottle of it topped with a vulgar gold lid shaped like a rose. All mixed up with nylon stockings and flimsy petticoats of black and cream, were blue and yellow plastic hair rollers with faded rust-coloured hair still trapped fast in the spikes. Corsets: trapped, skeletal pink bones in a silky material with rubber buttons dangling grotesquely from bits of elastic. Black-lace bras and French knickers to match and tucked down the sides were jars of face creams and tubes of embrocating ointments, lubricating jelly and an assortment of dildos. Neck-ties tied together with loops at the end to form some kind of restraining tether. Ties, belonging to Uncle Molly, Quinn deduced. And these Polaroid photographs! He twisted his head to glean the correct angle. Righted it. The contents of the case were ransacked as if they'd been gone through by a frenzied hand. Who had gone through Mrs Letty Jones' things? Had Mam's boys seen any of this? Then the tell-tale scent of perfume hit him and he knew. Knew that someone was still anointing the rooms with mam's sour-sweet and stale scent.

A voice called as Ted Molly climbed the stairs: How'y' doing, Quinn?

Ah... fine, fine so I am. Soon have your mam's treasures away from bringing back memories so we will... You've plenty to remember her by I know, but I'll save anything you might like to keep; there's some nice bars of soap here, lovely wrappings and sure you can still smell the lily of the valley… and here, there's a fine picture of you all with your dad in a silver frame, that'll take you back a bit, eh?

A Late-New-Year-Clearout is what Quinn called it. 'Start as you mean to go on, eh,' and he stacked redundant iron crates and feed troughs, metals signs, oil drums, buckets and canisters: a fine assortment of dross for the scrap-metal-man. Ted Molly and his brother got into the spirit of things and set to, helping. In the quickening dusk Quinn piled rotten old pallets and rags and over-worn work clothes, feed sacks and a variety of broken hutches onto the bonfire. The flames leapt high into the sky, sparks competing with the stars and while Ted Molly went in to fetch beer and crisps, Quinn heaved a suitcase into the middle and watched it fly with a dubious weight to land in the centre; the orange fiery tongues sucked and licked and the red leather turned a rich brown as Mam's past was eaten up.

A Double Whammy

There's one thing y'can say about me, I'm not self-pitying. OK, everyone can see what I am, it's not hidden away like mental health issues (can't say 'nuts' or 'crackers' or 'round the bend' anymore). I have a misshapen body because I'm abnormally undersized. I have a condition called dwarfism – 'a person with a usually genetic disorder resulting in atypically short stature and often disproportionate limbs; a midget – a small creature resembling a human, often having magical powers, appearing in legends and fairy tales.'

My name's Robert Roberts but they call me Bobi Two-Times.

No, as I said, I'm not self-pitying. In fact, things could be a lot worse and I count my blessings. Take the other day, I was travelling home on the bus up from Bangor to Carmel – I call Carmel 'the back of beyond; the heart of darkness', and a family of four sat opposite me. We don't see many black people up here in the sticks and I'd never seen a black albino before. Both small boys had cream-coloured hair tamed in little twists like bleached Brillo-pads.

I Googled 'blacks with white skin' on my phone right in front of them knowing they hadn't a clue, and found that in Africa, albinos are doomed; their persecution is based on the belief that 'certain body parts of albanistic people can transmit magical powers. Such superstition is exploited by witch-doctors who use body parts in rituals, concoctions and potions, claiming that its magic will bring prosperity, good luck, and fertility, to the user'.

To the witchdoctor more like it.

You can get albinism in birds which are soon pecked to death by the others. Fish, plants and animals, too. Can you imagine a white giraffe?

The dark brown parents tried to distract their children

from looking at me by pointing out the snow on top of the quarry workings. But I'm used to people staring because I have a 72-year-old face on a child's body. The kids were mesmerised; their four pink eyes couldn't look away.

For once though, I felt I had the better deal. No-one was going to kidnap and murder *me* to cut off *my* dick and use it to conjure up good luck and wealth for no buggering witchdoctors; the bas-tads!

P'raps that's why the black mum and dad have escaped to North Wales. These poor fuckers are in for double bad luck 'cause there's witchdoctors here, too.

Lilith

According to the villagers, Lilith Evans is a witch; most have a fear of her and stay clear away. Yet some come to leave butter, bread, milk and warm clothes in exchange for concoctions and tisanes. Curses fetch higher prices. Lilith lives on my land, as her family have always done, way up in the middle of the woods. Strangers don't know how to reach the witch, therefore, conduct their business via an old wooden toolbox placed just inside the kissing gate. The gate is situated halfway up the slope leading to the abandoned granite quarry. Eaten up by decades of bracken and brambles, the quarrymen's track is invisible and only Lilith and I know of the tunnel. We found it when we were children and used it for our clandestine meets.

When one is told not to mix with an undesirable half-witch-brood, best friends find a way. Lilith's ma kept toads and wild rabbits as pets; she fed feral cats which slinked and lounged about as if they owned the place. In those days, Lilith's ma used to receive visitors as if she were a duchess. Mother would not let me have a pet in the house. Our driveway was half a mile long, so nobody ever just dropped by. Father would have loved more company, but Mother said she liked the isolation; she said it gave us more time to be ourselves, to be who we should be. I craved time to spend with the Evans' who sat cuddled up in bundles of what seemed to be warm rags, listening to Ma tell stories of how she cured lumps, birthed babies, prepared a witch bottle and used a witch ball.

In hiding, Lilith and I used to watch, and listen for the footsteps trying to be quiet, the soft screech of the gate, and the clunk of the tool-box lid. That was in the mid-1950s. All these years later, some women still need specific doses and healing cream; and some have a wish to harm. The wooden box is still in use to leave begging-letters and notes. The gate still cries, quietly. A car engine late at night replaces the footfall.

Old age creeps up on us both. Lilith, less mobile than I, stops at the back door for a cup of tea sometimes. She doesn't chat much these days and I suspect she is a little demented, so we just pretend everything is as it was. And who am I to say it isn't, when it is I who mixes the potions and tinctures, makes the shapes, the poppets, the pin-pierced dolls.

Warm Flannelette

Quinn has moved on again, he has met Tiptoe and his family with whom he is ensconced for a while at their home, Fron Goch, helping out while Tiptoes' father, Leighton Hughes, is unwell.

Quinn did a bit of housekeeping at *Fron Goch*. Tiptoe and his father had not been too fussy over the years and their lodger offered to paint a couple of rooms.

Help y'self, Tiptoe said. You can choose the colours... Quinn had shaken his head at the lad's attitude and got on with it. I'll get on with it while you go and see your dad, he said.

Suits me! called Tiptoe as he flew like the wind down the track; the old Austin they used as if on air and making for the cottage hospital where his dad was recuperating after a second foot reconstruction.

The knock was dull, as if the caller didn't want to be on the errand.

What are you doing down here? Quinn asked the girl, Don't you live under *Bont Rhiwen?* He could have bitten off his tongue. I mean, how have you got down here? There aren't any buses today.

Walked.

All that way?

It's nothing. Easy. Straight across the fields.

The child was about fourteen and he could smell her from where he stood. Her family lived under the Rhiwen Bridge; they lived poorly and like animals in a couple of caravans and makeshift sheds. Quinn recognised her from the rounds when she came usually with one of the grandmothers to buy things from the van, nothing much just nets and cloth and sewing things. Tiptoe said he

134

heard they made stuff and sold it to a market stallholder near Caernarfon. Once when the ground was icy like glass, Quinn carried a bolt of seersucker and a bolt of gingham material for this child and left it where she indicated a little way from the hovel and when he looked back, an old lady had come out to help her and they leaned on one another as they slithered inside one of the sheds with their load. Whenever the van was up in that area, he tended to see one or more of them wandering about like displaced persons yet they never appeared to be looking for somewhere else to be. Quinn had a morbid curiosity about them, and one day when he had passed this child and four or five others of them collecting sticks in the woods, he took advantage of their absence and wandered along a portion of rail track towards *Bont Rhiwen*, as if to an onlooker, he was lost. He stepped carefully over discarded rubbish and stopped to gaze around and up as if it was all new to him, just so that he could get a little nearer. He stepped right under the bridge and smelled the sourness of the smoked-red brick.

When he got back to *Fron Goch*, they'd found Tiptoe's dad sitting behind his newspaper with his foot up, and Quinn had asked Tiptoe why they lived like that, that Frazer family of eleven or so people, three grandparents, her parents and siblings with a huge age range, all in such dereliction. Tiptoe said he didn't know but they'd always been there. Haven't they, dad?

Always, lad.

Always, Leighton?

Well, since the quarry train stopped running from *Chwarel Ddu.*

Quinn looked puzzled.

Once the train'd stopped after the quarry folded, the Frazers' pulled up a section of the track under the bridge

135

and squatted there and that's where they stayed! Been there for as long as I can remember. That right, Tiptoe?

S'right, dad.

But the place is dreadful! I've not *always* lived in such salubrious rooms, he said, smiling and waving his arm around, but I've never been anywhere as bad as that. It's not fit for dogs.

Dogs wouldn't stay...

Can't they be moved?

Tiptoe said, Council's offered but they don't want to...

Are they gypsies?

Hell, no! Don't let the gypos hear you say that. The gypos are a cut above, I can tell you, By.A.Long.Way!

Now the girl looked at Quinn and he noticed her red-ringed eyes.

Can I help at all?

Is Tiptoe here?

I'm afraid not.

His van's here, and she looked back into the yard as if he might be hiding there.

Yes.

Why isn't he here if his van's here?

He's... visiting his father in hospital.

I want to buy some cloth.

Today?

Yes.

Why today? We'll be up your way on Thursday.

She looked worried. Thursday's too late.

Quinn frowned, losing patience. Look here, he said, The van's not really open today...

I want some warm flannelette. Doesn't matter what colour... I don't think the colour matters...

Quinn got the keys and looked about him and hoped it wasn't some sort of trick. Hoped it wasn't a scheme to get him out of the house so he could be banged on the head and the whole place robbed... He walked towards the van and stopped, Look, he said, There's more stock in the barn there...

I don't want much, just enough to line my Nan's coffin. Coffin?

Yes, my Dandan made it but we didn't have time to line it before...

Oh, my goodness me...

My Nan died in the night and we haven't got the right cloth.

The scent of her dirty skin rose from her as she shook with grief. We didn't have the right cloth y'see...

We have just the thing, so we have, Quinn let her to the dark blue van. 'Tis a nice warm flannel the colour of a peach. She felt it between her dirty fingers and she wept quiet tears.

I will drive you home with this, said Quinn. He wouldn't hear her protests and drove her to the shacks. The late afternoon was pleasant, even as they approached this wretched place. He made to get out and take her to her door.

I'm ok, here...

I'd like to see you in so I would, just this once...

She said nothing and he walked her over the mess and a tin can rattled as he tried to avoid it and a dog barked once. The caravan door opened as she put a foot on the top step and she went in and looked back at him. A small wave of acknowledgement from someone fluttered from behind her as the door closed.

Quinn was filled with a sense of melancholy.

Would anyone care enough to line his coffin with warm flannel, the colour of a peach?

Reading Between the Lines

My name is Cornelia Fox (Nell). I've always thought of myself as being of sound mind, a level-headed person, but for the past six/seven months I have been experiencing a most improbable situation. I have hinted as much to three people: Jessie Merchant who has become a close friend during the eight years she's been helping me in the house, Dr Stanley Peach, friend, psychiatrist and colleague of my late husband, Dr James Fox, and my GP, Dr Harriet Lacey.

I haven't been totally honest when speaking of my concerns because they sound so bizarre even to me! I just said my memory and mind were playing tricks on me, and occasionally I was hearing things. Stan and Dr Lacey suggested I wrote an account from when these episodes started to affect me. Stan said a perfectly sensible explanation might emerge from opening up my mind by putting pen to paper. He said he'd take a look at what I'd written and we would go from there.

I am now so frightened by developments that I will do as he says so that some explanation can be found.

And I can stop thinking I'm losing my mind.

There is never a true beginning to anything; even at the haphazard and precarious moment of conception, one's beginning is already lost in myriad generations and histories. But I will start at my birth.

I was the second child of my schoolteacher father, Thomas Mantell, and my mother, Catherine, a nurse. We lived in a little granite quarrying hamlet surrounded by mountains, accessed down a steep track, which if followed, soon came to the beach and the Irish Sea. My sister, Dinah, was five years older than I and was confined to a wheelchair. That is how I identified her – my sister who lived in a wheelchair. My parents' lives revolved around her, and I never got used to being secondary. I guess I was jealous of her, of the attention she got from them, from everyone, really. Aunts and uncles and all four of my grandparents doted on her. They overcompensated I suppose for her disability. I know I acted naughtily at times, aggravating and teasing her just to make them notice me.

She drowned when I was six years old; strapped in her wheelchair, she tumbled off the little stone jetty when the tide was in. I believe I tried to rescue her, but the weight of the wheelchair took her down before my father could jump in and save us both. When I was feeling sorry for myself and something of a martyr, I sometimes felt as if I should have drowned and then they could have concentrated on her without my presence; and then I would think, No! it's my turn to have the attention now.

Needless to say, no-one in our family spoke about the tragedy in front of me, and due to my age, it subsequently retreated to the back of my mind. Because the story did not see the light of day; it drowned also, in a deep, dark watery place.

Writing this down brings to mind how it felt after Dinah died; even though she was dead, there was still an almost tangible presence. She seemed to be there, sitting in her wheelchair always looking at me.

As young as I was, I know my parents took good care of me, but they did not like me.

I have laid out the basics as far as I can remember of our time in Nant Carreg, the tiny place where we lived until I was almost eight, until my father became headmaster of a senior school sixty miles away.

I must now move on to the present to record what I have been going through for the past months.

It was anniversary time, April, May. Foxy had died a year ago and my mother, a couple of years previously. I suppose it influenced my mood and brought on a mild melancholia.

139

Mother's estate had been finalised, but recently I've been looking at what she left behind – certificates of all her golfing successes, old photographs, letters – not to be advised perhaps when one is feeling low – but I wanted to deal with her things finally. Another step forward I thought. Mother and I had never been very close, but she deserved to have her possessions sorted and disposed of in the most appropriate way. There was little I wanted materially except for photographs of my parents, sister and grandparents and those depicting the life we lived before I left for university. The black and white images of us at Nant Carreg were captivating and I decided to put these on one side. I have no family now so having these is a tenuous link to the family we once were when we lived in North Wales.

I think that was my undoing – letting those photographs of Nant Carreg take me back, they seemed to draw me into them until I could smell the quarry dust on the sea air, smell the goats as they tiptoed, and the sheep as they nibbled on the grassy slopes, the ferns and bracken with their fresh-green and heavy scent. I could feel the little pebbles under my bare feet on the seashore. I even experienced the heaviness of Dinah's wheelchair as I helped to push her along.

Never having any particular interest before, Nant Carreg now seemed to draw me. How ridiculously weird is that?

Out of the blue, I said to myself: Drive into Wales, it'll be a nice change. Now, where had that come from? I rarely set foot over the border. I suddenly thought, why? Why did I always shy away from Wales? Even when Foxy and Stan played on the most beautiful golf links and courses, I made excuses not to join them for their weekends…

What made me decide to go there, I do not know. It became the last place I eventually wanted to go. That's what these bouts of depression do to me – make me think about something positive that might get me out and about, then soon after, my thoughts turn negative, uncertain and want to stay at home.

I told Jessie I might take a couple of days break-away. 'Wales, I thought. It's not too far…'

'That's a nice idea, Nell; going down memory lane, are you?'

I hadn't thought about it like that at all. But why not?

'Yes, Jessie, something like that I suppose; to tell the truth I don't really know where I'm going; it'll be an adventure!'

We both laughed when she said, 'Ah, Famous Five – Nell Goes off into Darkest Wales.'

As I packed up my mini estate the following day. I spoke to myself again – stay as long as you like, there's no-one waiting here for you. Take your sketch book, paints, and books on your to-read list. Walking boots.

Since Foxy died, I've tried to keep myself busy: art classes, Pilates, yoga, hospital visiting, helping in a charity-shop – that sort of thing. Not being in any kind of a rush (in fact I had in the back of my mind that I could turn around and come home, or go somewhere else, should I want), I dawdled.

Now loaded up, the idea seemed silly, and I was already feeling that I didn't want to go anywhere at all, but then Jessie arrived, and I knew I'd feel even sillier if I changed my mind and started to unload.

'Jessie,' I said, before I lost courage. 'I'll be off in about an hour. It's only for a few days. I'll phone this evening.'

Travelling along the North Wales coast with the sea on my right, I came upon the hills and mountains of Conwy and the Penmaenmawr granite quarry. The mountain's greyness, its bare rock and its majestic standing, reminded me of the two small sister quarries to which I was heading. I could sense a homecoming, but that is totally absurd as I hardly remember the place and had never ventured this far along the coast before. It was then that I thought how strange – Wales was a stone's-throw from the Wirral, so why had my parents never ventured back to where we lived? I had a vague sense without knowing why, that our time there was an episode hardly ever mentioned and certainly a destination never to be entertained. I realised I had unconsciously accepted that it was a place we didn't go to. But for goodness' sake, both my parents had died, and I'd lived an adult life for almost fifty years. How had their reluctance skulked so solidly at the back of my mind? Silently, yet loud enough for me to have never crossed over the border into Wales?

After scrutinizing the AA map, and checking my route, it was about an hour before I saw the sign to Llithfaen and travelled along enjoying the views of the Rival mountains ahead. Arriving at Pistyll, I turned sharp right at the little crossroads and followed the narrow road up and up until I came to a plateau and the most extraordinary view of the widest sky ahead, and then I saw the road incline taking me down to Nant Carreg.

Oh, my goodness, it was like travelling in the Alps – a sheer drop to my left where I stopped to see the little village below. Suddenly, I seemed to be someone else, looking at the place with their eyes. I became that other person there and then and suddenly I wasn't sure who I was; but I knew that Nant Carreg knew me and wanted me to be there. I had the strange feeling that it was beckoning me.

Slowly I drove down and reached the small car park. The silence seemed tangible and hit me as soon as I opened the car door. I stood for minutes, just absorbing the peace.

Both scarred quarries stood like sentinels, with their feet in the sea. In between, the little hamlet faced the horizon. Its old chapel was being spruced up. A notice board advertised cottages to let, and I found myself booking into No. 3 Ocean View Terrace, from where I could see the house we had lived in at the end of Quarry View Terrace. The hamlet looked pretty much the same as it did in our old photographs. The old Co-op store stood with its roof in a bad state and held together by stone walls. The pigsty had been converted into a small café and craft shop selling pottery and hand-made corn-dollies. I walked past and stood to look at the shoreline below. From our old photographs it seemed that little had changed – there was little *to* change. The only sign of modernity since we lived there was a telephone box.

I suppose it was natural that being there brought back memories, no matter how sketchy, but I was not expecting to actually feel as if I were back there, in person so to speak, with the sound of crushing stone, the constant movement of the sea shifting up the pebbled beach, the hoot of boats waiting to come in and be loaded up, the quarry machinery in the background. As I scrambled down to the water's edge, I smelled the combination of the salty sea and the ghostly granite dust.

The small stone jetty had been removed. It was here that I regressed sixty or so years as I saw my parents, hysterical, and my sister strapped in her wheelchair lying side down on the shingle, her straw-coloured hair now dark, slathered over her open-mouthed face.

Eventually I turned to make my way back where I indulged in a nice cream tea at the café. I people-watched but felt totally distanced from them, as if I were viewing them from another place altogether. It was a very strange feeling which wouldn't go away. Telling myself not to be so silly, I collected the keys to No. 3 Ocean View, and drove my car from the car park to unload my bags. I was surprised to find the door already unlocked.

The small two-up-two-down cottage was pretty cosy once the heating came on and suddenly, I felt that this was right. I had made a good decision to come here and settle for a couple of days in the peace and quiet. After enjoying a ready-meal and half a bottle of decent wine, I finished off with cheese and biscuits. I leafed through the guidebooks, and planned a walk the next day. I would take my sketch book with me.

Then I remembered Jessie, and ambled along to join a small queue at the telephone kiosk. A woman looked helplessly at her mobile phone. No signal in this god-forsaken place, she told me.

Jessie was pleased to hear that I had arrived and was staying a couple of nights.

'It'll do you good,' she said. 'You've not been yourself, lately.'

I didn't know what to say. I didn't know I had not 'been myself' lately.

She then said, 'Is there someone with you?'

'Someone with me? No. Why?'

'I can hear someone talking over you.'

'It must be a crossed line,' I said, at the same time thinking, no-one has crossed lines these days.

'It's a god-forsaken place,' I chuckled. 'All this granite and we're deep in a valley…'

'Take care, Nell.' She sounded concerned. Dear old Jess.

Back in the cottage, a weariness overtook me quite suddenly, so I locked up, filled a hot-water bottle, and went up to my bedroom where I had started to unpack. Initially I thought the room was spacious for such a small cottage, but now it felt as if it were occupied by someone other than me, and that something had taken over my space. I experienced a sense of claustrophobia and I had the distinct feeling that I was not alone. How ridiculous, I thought, and opened the window wide. I put my head out and took some deep breaths. The night air was sweet and very quiet. I heard a solitary sheep cry, and two owls talking to each other. I heard the goats moving on the hillside, their dainty tiptoeing causing the slipping and sliding of tiny stones.

After all this time, they were still roaming the hillside, their strong scent catching at the back of my throat.

I didn't have a good night's sleep; I put it down to a strange bed in a strange place. It wasn't a cold night, but I woke in the early hours shivering, to find the duvet had been folded back down to my waist. A really neat fold.

Daylight – and I woke to a clatter of things falling over and found my bedside table contents on the floor. A stack of books must have overbalanced, but I wondered why they hadn't fallen before now. What had disturbed them? As I put the books back, I heard someone cough which un-nerved me. A similar sound came from outside and when I looked out of the window, some sheep had wandered down into the gardens. Now and again, they made sharp small sounds as if they were choking. For goodness' sake, I told myself. Get out into the fresh air and walk off these fancy imaginings.

After a shower, I put on my walking boots, packed my sketch book, and went out into the glorious spring day. Once I was outside the cottage, I felt totally different. I had left that unsettling atmosphere behind.

As a child, I never strayed beyond the little square and the beach, so exploring the circular walk which took me all morning because I stopped to draw and enjoy the view, I felt as if I had discovered new territory. A place I had never been to before.

When I got back into the cottage I felt suddenly right back to where I was as a six-year-old little girl, with my ever-present sister, Dinah. Dinah seemed to stay with me for the rest of the day, which I spent strolling among the heathered hillside and wandering on the beach. I stood for a long time by the remains of the old jetty and of course, my sister's death was on my mind. The demolished jetty's foundation stumps looked like guttered candles and of

145

course took me straight to the day of Dinah's death. I expected to re-live the accident, but a battle taking place in my mind would not let me into such a long-standing memory. For that I was grateful; it would not be very helpful to dwell on it.

That night, I was physically tired after the unaccustomed scrambling over rocks and along the shoreline. I read a while before dozing off. I slept deeply but about 3am I was woken by a strong smell of seawater, and sitting in the chair was my sister, Dinah. I lay petrified and thought I might stop beathing. Horrified and disoriented until I realised there was no-one in the room at all. I peered through the half-light to see the chair piled untidily with my rucksack and clothes.

Good heavens! I thought, What a stupid thing to think.

The smell of wet sea-weed was very strong though which un-nerved me a little, and when I got out of bed, I found my feet standing on a wet rug.

Now I felt a rising panic in my chest which threatened to turn into hysteria.

This is madness! I almost shouted it. This had not been a good idea after all. What on earth made me think it was?

Convincing myself that I must have spilled some water, I rushed to get out into the open air. I might leave today; I continued to talk to myself. Two nights of strange happenings in this cottage was enough. Yes, I would leave late afternoon and be in the sanity of my own home by evening.

I found the gift shop within the café and was pleasantly surprised to find good quality pottery by a local artist. I purchased a salad bowl and some serving dishes in a muted mustard-colour with a glazed interior of earth-green. I immediately felt better and when the sun shone on the spectacular landscape, and I saw families walking about

146

happily, I decided that a night-terror and imagination had got the better of me.

I would stay one more night.

Like most people, I'd had nightmares where I could actually feel someone sitting on my bed, actually hear a voice, hear myself scream, even. And then take a few moments to realise it was only a dream.

But that third night was an exception I can hardly put into words. At about 2 am I awoke suddenly to the sound of someone breathing very near me. Laboured breathing. The fear I experienced pinned me down so that I took at least 30 seconds to move. As I did so I felt icy, wet hands disturbing the bedclothes and find their way around my neck. The hands were not very strong and my strength, fuelled by fear, managed to free me as I made to sit up. The sound of both sets of breathing filled the room and as my eyes became accustomed to the dark, I saw a shape leave the room through the open door. Which I knew I had closed before settling down.

I put on the light and lay there awake until about 5 am.

No matter how I tried to think that this was my imagination. I could not. The bedclothes and my top were still damp where the hands had crept towards my neck.

Am I mentally disturbed – am I losing my mind? I thought. I had just experienced the impossible. I felt helpless and wretched.

Once daylight broke and I'd hastily packed up my things, I made up my mind to seek help – see Stan when I got back, and hope he would be able to wipe out all I'd been through in the last few days.

I was not at all surprised that I should feel a presence of long-gone people, of senses, of atmosphere. I was in a place where

147

I spent almost eight years of my life as a child, and understood that many of the memories might be distorted as they emerged, rendering them unreliable. But I was not prepared for those hauntings to accompany me home to Altrincham.

I tried to pinpoint the first indication. It was when I started to pack up my car. It isn't a big vehicle but there was plenty of room for my things on the way to Wales; try as I might, I could hardly fit in all my stuff, and when I returned to the car to collect my easel, it seemed that something had been moved causing a further difficulty. Obviously, I was imaging this, and eventually, gave up and simply shoved my waterproofs and walking boots in the back, re-arranging the two boxes of pottery I'd bought in the shop, and set off. It was to take about two and a half hours with extra time to stop and buy provisions from the local farm shop.

It was a treat to shop there. I filled my basket with lots of fresh veg, nice cuts of meat, and ready-to-cook coq au vin and moussaka. Perhaps I shouldn't have bought so much as I had to haphazardly balance the bags on top of the pottery.

The journey was uneventful and already I felt that I'd over-reacted, that somehow my mind was playing tricks on me.

When I got home, I found items in my shopping which had not been chosen by me. Two tins of baked beans, bourbon biscuits and a box of chocolates. Baked beans? Who doesn't have a few tins always on standby? Why would I add such mundane goods?

I then decided it was just a silly mix-up and sudden loss of concentration. I'd been on quite an emotional journey whether I liked to admit it or not. Forget it and get on with everyday life for goodness' sake.

To do this, it felt imperative that I took some control.

Draw a line under the past few days and put all this Nant Carreg nonsense out of my mind; it obviously wasn't doing me any good.

The first step was to pack up all my mother's papers and photographs; put them in a box and dispose of them once and for all. I didn't need any reminders of what I think I experienced at Nant GCarreg.

It took longer than I thought, but eventually the deed was done. Everything neatly stacked away. I felt it was a goodbye to the past.

I had today's living to enjoy.

I closed the door on the room and all the unpleasantness it held.

I was appalled when I entered the room the following day after Jessie had gone home, I found my mother's papers back on my desk looking as if someone had riffled through them. The box of photographs was opened and twelve of them were laid out as if someone was going to start playing Patience. Primarily they were of Dinah and me, ones I had scrutinised in the days before my trip. Six black-and-white images of Dinah before I was born. She looked very happy, with wide smiles and her face screwed up with laughter, and the ubiquitous parents or grandparents standing behind or alongside her wheelchair like guardian angels. Three photos of Dinah with the infant me, in her arms. Again, the guardian angels hovered. The rest were of us both in later years. Me, always as if to move off and run, or throw a ball, and one with me trying to swirl a hula-hoop around my waist. Dinah's body, strapped in the wheelchair, seemed to sag.

Looking closer, I couldn't rid myself of the thought that there were subtle changes in our expressions – particularly one of her looking at me with sly hostility. And one of me, fixing her with spiteful glee.

149

I don't know what upset me most, the unsettling effect the images conjured up, or the fact that they'd been removed from the box and placed strategically on my desk so that I should not miss them. It was as if someone was trying to tell me a story in pictures.

Did Jessie know something I did not? Had she taken to prying? Disturbing my papers? Impossible. I would trust Jessie with my life.

This most frightening and disturbing incident should have made me burn everything there and then: papers, photographs, sketches, in fact anything that had connections with that place, Nant Carreg.

Apart from the obvious conclusion that someone other than Jess had access to my house, it soon became apparent that there was a poltergeist in my home – a mean-minded thing. A childish spirit, who wanted to make itself felt and known to me, it drew my attention to many small things, things which made no sense. For instance, I found tea-bags split open and leaves littering the worktop in my kitchen. A carton of milk in the sink, having been emptied.

When I found myself getting up to answer the doorbell again, finding no-one there for the third time that day, I felt wretched. There was something wrong with me. Was I having a nervous breakdown? Was I going mad? These provocative thoughts, over which I felt I had no control, led me backwards into a fit of depression.

My poltergeist (as I had started to call it) then had a field-day; it really went for me when I was down. My bedclothes were hauled off me when I slept, and I woke to the sound of taps running, and my bedside bookmark in the wrong place.

A week of this behaviour made me mention it to Jessie; she of course noticed none of these things, saying I must have moved such and such a book, left a light on when I

150

know I switched it off, and said that our minds can play tricks on us when we least expect it. Ride it out, Nell, she said. Ride it out. But when she arrived one day and saw that my tins of food had been emptied from the cupboard and placed on the kitchen table – placed to spell out the word, 'ME', even she said she was alarmed. But I'm not sure if she was worried about my poltergeist, or about my state of mind.

'I'll stay a couple of nights with you,' she offered. 'Just a couple of nights to see how things go.'

I could tell that she thought my mind was unsteady. And before she could suggest it, I told her I would go and see my GP.

Dr Lacey was very understanding, gave me some medication and some advice. Write things down, she said. Write how you feel each day, what occurs that you find disquieting. Write down as you go to bed, that you have switched off lights room by room, turned off all taps. She even suggested I take a photograph of my living room and desk, so that I could compare it the next day if something seemed different. I thought that was a bit extreme, so chose to ignore it, but when I found my walking shoes soaking in the kitchen sink the next morning, minute pebbles and sand from Nant Carreg having settled around them like a small beach, I wished I had done just that. At least I'd have some proof that the sink was clear the night before, and my shoes were in the cupboard.

Who could have put my shoes in the sink? Where had the pebbles and sand come from? The smell of saltwater?

I stood stock-still for more than a minute. My breath remained tight in my chest. My eyes slowly moved around the room. There was someone here. I knew it without a shadow of doubt.

My consciousness slowly told me what I knew. What I had known for some time.

Dinah was here in my house.

151

I can't believe I've actually written that down! If anyone reads it, they'd know I am losing my mind. They'll have no doubt that I'm going mad.

That's when I became really frightened.

The thought that I had abandoned reality and acknowledged that Dinah was here with me, left me very scared indeed, and that's when I decided to contact Stan Peach at the hospital. I underwent a series of psychiatric examinations. I didn't tell him everything; I just said I was feeling low, and that my imagination was getting the better of me. He coaxed me to giving a few examples, so I told him about the doorbell ringing with no-one there, about the lights being switched on when I knew I'd turned them off. I told them about all these incidents, but I could not voice the reality of what I now knew – that Dinah had come home with me from Nant Carreg.

Ah,' Stan said. 'Imagination. It's as real as fact at times… It's a very powerful thing.'

In line with Dr Lacey, one thing he recommended was that I should write down everything I experienced: 'From the very beginning of feeling unsettled, Nell,' Stan said. I suspected he meant everything I 'think' I experienced.

But that was when I decided to do as they suggested. I had nothing to lose, I thought, so why not start from the very beginning as Stan mentioned. Of course, I had no intention of letting the doctors see everything that I wrote down because it was so fantastical. But it may throw some light on things in my own mind.

I felt as if I were actually getting somewhere with the experiment of writing all this down. Re-reading what I'd recorded, putting pen to paper helped me to focus and to acknowledge that perhaps I had imagined some of the incidents, for example, did I start to clean my walking boots, forget about them, and find them as I left them – in the sink as if abandoned on a sandy beach? Did I hear the doorbell ring so many times? The more I thought about this, the more comfortable I became, and so told Jessie.

'I think my mind has been playing tricks on me, Jess. Some of the time anyway!'

'That can happen, Nell, so I've heard, especially if you've been through an emotional time.'

Well, I know I lost my mother, and then my husband within a couple of years. Of course, losing Foxy was absolutely dreadful, but I think I've coped as well as anyone else I know.

'I thought I'd coped well, after Foxy,' I told her.

'On the surface, yes,' she replied. 'On the surface. But you never know what lurks just below. Oh, and don't forget you went on that little break to Wales – who knows what that brought up from your childhood.'

Jessie was stating what any amateur psychologist says when there seems to be no reasonable explanation for mysterious goings-on, but none of it made any sense to me.

'You're probably right, Jess.' I agreed with her because I had nothing to say that made any sense, and nothing that disputed what she suggested, but even after accepting that I may have been mistaken about some of the incidents, I know myself well enough to know that I was not imagining everything that was occurring in my own home.

I was trying to act normally, trying to say things Jess wanted to hear. Trying to deny what I knew to be true.

But where did that leave me? With the paradox of all this being in my imagination and the actual belief of Dinah's existence in my house.

Now I've acknowledged that Dinah is here, it seems as if she watches everything I do. Dinah, my sister who died almost fifty years ago.

How on earth did I come to this conclusion as if it were the most natural thing to be happening? All I know is that I must put up with her until this account is written.

Then I'll concentrate on getting rid of her once and for all.

Dinah doesn't speak to me the whole time she watches me write, but she bristles when I write about getting rid of her. I feel her move agitatedly as if she wants to convey something. No matter how many times I look at her she only stares at me, willing me to understand. I've become so used to her being with me, I've started to talk conspiratorially to her in whispers.

And here she is now, she sits just alongside me watching as I put down my story.

I should not have gone back to Nant Carreg. I know that now, but I also know that I had no control over my sister's visitations.

Before I prepared for bed, I re-read the written words which gives me an assurance that I've been accurate in what I remember. Try as I might, I cannot explain what I experienced. I just have to accept that my dead sister has come to pay me a visit after fifty years. In putting pen to paper, I'd done as I was asked, but I still felt there was some unfinished business to sort out – but what? And how on earth am I going to share this with anyone else? Surely, I will be found insane.

That's when I decided that I would show no-one. I will deny any of my previous complaints and admit that I was imagining it all. There is nothing wrong with me; my sister is not here in my home.

And no-one will see what I have written.

Looking around the room, there was no sound, and no sight of anyone or anything that shouldn't be there. I tidied my desk, put away my pens, notepads, emptied my wastepaper bin, and placed my handwritten manuscript in an envelope. I would lock it away, or might burn it.

Having made this decision, I went to bed feeling a heavy weight had been removed from my mind.

I would sleep well and tomorrow would be a new day.

I woke feeling refreshed, as if my mind had been cleared and the past few months had happened to someone else.

Having a round of golf planned and a stint at the charity shop, I was also looking forward to seeing Stan, he was coming for drinks at about 6pm and I would tell him what I'd discovered – that I had been through a very strange few months but now all was well, he'd been right all along, my imagination was playing tricks on me.

I would keep the secret of my sister's presence to myself.

Until I could think of a way to get rid of her.

Nothing could have prepared me for what awaited my eyes when I got into my study. My desk was strewn this time with my papers. Dinah had underlined my last sentence *'Until I could think of a way to get rid of her.'*

She'd scratched out some of my words and replaced them. It was a child-like, spiteful way of destroying my own record of what I remember happened to her: the way the wheelchair had mysteriously slid away to the jetty's edge and into the sea.

Horrified and frightened I felt for the chair behind me. I had to sit down. I had to look at what was altered. Where I'd written 'my story', it had been changed to 'our story'. When I wrote about my visit to Nant Carreg where I thought all this had begun, many 'I's' had been replaced with 'we' as if I had not been alone; as if someone had actually been there with me. 'My parents' had become 'our parents'. And the time I was phoning Jess, the 'I' had been changed to 'we'. So, she was with me in that telephone box? Jess had been right; she had heard someone talking over me…

Where I recalled the awful accident of Dinah's death, I saw a messy group of words, lots of crossing out, the pen having scored through the paper. The words blended into one another and as I tried to make sense of them, my recollection of how her wheelchair had slid slowly then quicker towards the jetty's edge, appeared as a flashback as clear as daylight.

I had tampered with the brake.

It had first been tightened by my father and I could feel the resistance of it as I grappled to loosen it – I could feel the tough rubber hand of the brake, the metal, my sister's hand, her fingers grabbing mine as we both careered towards the sea. I saw it as if it were happening now.

The shock took my breath away and when it returned, it came in short gasps, my hand at my throat, clutching my necklace until it broke, glass beads flying in all direction, bouncing on the parquet floor. And that's when I heard Dinah laugh. Both an excited and then nervous laugh as if she was uncertain – as if she'd gone too far.

I had to face it; I had tried to kill my sister. I had killed her.

I released the brake; I feel it now as it smoothly, easily gives way, I feel it slipping away from me. My hand entwined with Dinah's and her other hand clutching my arm in a grip of iron – neither of us letting go in the terror of what was happening. That's why she came back with me to my home – to punish me in the only way she knew how.

Hearing my mother's alarmed call, my father's running, the noise was horrendous with all the shouting from others who could see what was about to happen, the sound of the wheels as they picked up speed towards the jetty's edge.

I saw Dinah's face. Her eyes full of dislike and puzzlement. And fury. She was furious with me. She was panic-struck and she screamed, shouted. I couldn't hear above the cries. Mine and hers as she shot out words, spittle like sea foam on her lips and chin. And then I realized the scream was real. It was as if for the first time, a bright light shone on the actual happening as if it were a film shot.

Again, I felt the cold sea-water taking us down. I saw her mouth open as if she were still shouting at me and the water rushed about my ears thrashing and thundering.

Being light in weight, I rose as she loosened her grip.

My father could not save her. No-one could have saved a heavily built child strapped tight in her wheelchair.

Once I stopped screaming, the silence in my study is as loud as the cacophony of the few minutes it took to kill my sister.

It was the first time I had the strength to accept with certainty that Dinah's presence in my living room had been as natural as anything I ever knew. And Dinah was still here.

But how had I missed the fact that I had a hand in killing my sister? A deliberate hand that released the brake in order to kill her so that I could be the focus of my family's attention. It was too shocking to accept, but there it is. A vignette before my very eyes.

What on earth was I to do? This put a new slant on things.

I cancelled Stan's visit. I did the same with Jess. I needed time to sort out my dreadful thoughts.

Unwilling to accept the revelation, and so that I won't wonder later if I imagined the horrendous disclosure, I wrote on the page *'I killed my sister, Dinah'*.

Unable to take all this in, I went back to bed to escape what I reluctantly learned. I hoped I would wake and find all this to be a nightmare. It must have been a nightmare. It must have been.

As I shut the door, I heard her shuffle into a corner.

It took me two days to build up enough courage to go back into that room.

My sister has not finished with me yet!

My account was laid out, page after page of my writing and Dinah's scrawl.

On the page where I'd written, *'I killed my sister, Dinah'* she added, 'So you did. I won't forgive you, you evil child. But what you don't know is that I was about to murder you. I had released the wheelchair brake enough to move it slowly down the jetty's incline, and where I knew you would attempt to play the heroine and try to stop it. I intended to entice you to the edge of the jetty where I was to push you in the deep water. You were starting to take away the attention I thrived on.

'I failed to kill you because you were stronger than I was.

'You took my life.

'I will now stay with you forever, to share yours.'

The Infant Jesus

15th December 2020

'So, you're going to work in the Loony Bin are you?'

'Nan, please don't call it that.'

'That's what it is. What it was.'

'It was also a Paupers' House and a Workhouse as you well know, but things have changed since the dark ages. For heaven's sake, just call it St Jude's, that's easy enough to say.'

If anyone needed St Jude's intervention just now, it was Nan – Nan wasn't a complete hopeless case, but she was getting more unreasonable every day.

'After all that training, why are you not a proper nurse? Or a doctor, even?'

'It's what I want, Nan. One doctor in the house is enough, don't y'think?'

'Hm.' Magda McSweet looked disgruntled. 'I can't understand even now what made you give up that good job with the college, so I can't.'

'I've told you. It's just something I've always wanted to do, and do before I get too old.'

'Too old? How old are you now?'

'I'll be thirty-four on Christmas Eve, Nan. And that's not too old to change direction, now, is it?'

'I don't know why you're asking me. No-one takes any notice of what I say these days.'

'Are you not even going to wish me luck on my first day, at all?'

Nan looked sideways at her grandchild. 'Aye, indeed I do wish you luck, lovey. All the luck in the world. Here take this and buy something nice for yourself.' She held out a €1.

Vinny McSweet took it.

'Thanks. Thanks a lot, Nan.'

Buy something nice for myself? Fat chance! I wonder how long it'll be before Nan needs to go into somewhere to be cared for. She gets worse by the day.

'Will I see you next week, then y'crotchety old rascal?'

'God willing, God willing.' She crossed herself. 'If I'm spared, if I'm spared.'

He left, smiling.

His wife was a doctor in the modern state-of-the-art psychiatric hospital just outside Sligo. Vinny chose St Jude's, which is now a little cottage hospital for those who were deemed harmless but beyond any more psychiatric help. It's a ten-minute drive from home and situated a stone's throw away from the Marian Shrine in Knock. Dotted about the parish were smaller churches: St Bartholomew, St Mary Magdalena and St Concepta to name a few. St Concepta was the McSweet family church.

'I don't know how long St Jude's will manage to keep going,' the charge nurse told Vinny on his first shift. 'What with cuts, you know... the financial climate. But at the moment we're blessed with the way things are. I dread to think where these old souls'd go if we ever closed. It's more like a Care Home. In fact, we call everyone 'home-helpers' here, then the residents don't think they're in a psychiatric ward and forever asking to go home.' She talked as they left the office. 'Let me show you around. Knock's fortunate that there's somewhere for its mentally impaired locals to end their days. But some of them I can tell you, are no more impaired than a lot of old folk out there seem to be!'

Vinny thought of his Nan when the nurse said that.

'Take these,' she said. 'To the ones in the Day Room.' A large, bright room with seven or eight easy chairs facing the TV, which was silent yet showed a nature programme of violent proportions. A nicely shaped Christmas tree with gaudy lights stood in the corner and every festive decoration imaginable was dotted about the room. Quietly sung carols drifted from the radio.

'Here, Terry, meet our new home-helper, Vinny.'

Terry saluted and said, 'Yes, sir.'

'And Mick. We have two Micks here,' she said. 'And a Micky. This is Mick Shelly.'

'Hyia, Mick, how're doing?'

'Splendid today, thanks.'

'And then here's Mary. Mary McAllister.'

'I've got a Christmas baby,' Mary told Vinny, hugging a model of the Infant Jesus wrapped in a crocheted multi-coloured blanket.

'Have you now, Mary. That's interesting. And how old is he?'

'Sixty-five come Christmas Eve. His name's Vincent.'

'Ah-ha. Sixty-five, you say? Hmm.'

Mary eased open the blanket to show the plaster-cast baby in his swaddling clothes.

'And he has my name too, so he has.' Vinny showed Mary his name-badge. 'A bonny boy you have there.'

Mary McAllister fixed him and his badge with a stare, which slowly changed to a frown as she opened her mouth to speak, but the charge nurse had moved on to the next chair. 'And this is Micky. Micky Lane.'

'Hello there, Micky Lane,' Vinny put his hand out.

'Fuck off you.'

And so it went on.

December 24th 1955 10:30pm

'What're y'shouting for, Mary? Why're y'screaming like this? Will I get the doctor t'you? Dear Jesus, Mary and Joseph! Hush, for God's sake. How long have you been

161

here? Shouldn't we be at the vigil? That's where I should be going but I came looking for you.'

Two fifteen-year-old, terrified teenagers huddled at the back of the cattle shed at the McSweet farm. Fifteen-year-old Mary McAllister didn't know how she came to be in this mess of blood and water and slippery stuff being pushed out from her private parts by what felt like the contents of her brother's tool-box: pliers, a wrench, clamps and a rusty saw. Eventually she shoved out a scrap, the likes of a small, skinned rabbit.

'Oh, my dear Lord.' Vince McSweet looked appalled. 'What – what's all this?'

The new mother could hardly utter a word. 'I-I don't know, Vince. I don't know.' She shook violently. 'I don't understand,' and she lowed just as a cow does when she is in distress. Familiar with farmyard births, Vince had a sense of what to do but hesitated as he held the knife awkwardly. 'Hush hush hush,' is all he could say. Soon, he severed the rabbit from his school friend and was surprised to see it move. 'It's a baby, so it is. A real human baby.'

'No, no,' Mary moaned and started keening. 'No, dear God, no.'

Vince could make neither head nor tail of what she was saying as a cacophony of sounds filled the barn. Cattle stomped and stamped. The carthorse next door kicked and whinnied excitedly, and Mary keened like a banshee. Her face was burning to the touch, yet pale as death as she fell silent. It couldn't be less like that stable stall of two-thousand years ago. For the love of God Almighty, help us.

Then she started up again in an eerily sinister voice, the words struggling out between her clenched teeth. 'No, Declan. No, y'mustn't. Y'can't. Mammy'll...' It was about eight months ago and now the pain brought it all back. Her brother. Her brother, Declan. 'I don't want to go to Hell,

162

Declan. Dec, don't...' And the wailing started up again, this time, very quietly and as if she knew no-one was listening.

What to do now? First Vince sat and held her hand and told her that she had a baby boy.

'He doesn't look long for this world, Mary. There's nothing of him.' And he rubbed the tiny chest with straw and an old towel, then held him by the ankles as he would a new-born lamb and swung him till the baby made sounds.

'Will I try to give him milk? From the cow?'

The milk dribbled down the baby's cheeks and chin as Vince dipped his little finger and tried to ease some into its mouth.

We must try and baptise the little fella, Mary. We have to save his tiny soul, and Vince proceeded to make the sign of the cross on his forehead: 'I baptize thee – what'll you call him, Mary? What name'll you give him?

'I don't care. Take him away, Vince, please. Please take him away.'

'He has to be named, Mary, you can't just...'

Mary turned her head and put her hand over her face.

So, it was up to the boy, Vince. By now he couldn't think straight and named the baby Vincent. It was the only name his brain could come up with. He wrapped him up tight in the towel and watched as the baby's face took on a bit of colour.

'I tell you what. I'll look out for him. Make sure he's safe, leave him where he can be found and cared for properly, for it's sure we can't let on we have anything to do with it. Not in a month of Sundays, so we can't!' He sat in the now quiet barn, looking at his friend. 'How will y'get home, Mary? Can you move? Walk?'

Opening her eyes, Mary whispered for him to leave her

163

there for a while. 'I'll make my way home as if I've been to Midnight Mass.'

'We'll be missed, Mary; we never miss Mass.'

'Shall we say we were at the back of the church. A bit late getting there?'

'Aye. Yes, what else can we do? You sure you don't want me to call someone for help?' She shook her head slowly and tears just flowed unhindered. 'What'll I do with the baby? Vince? What'll I do with Vincent?'

Vince picked up the child and held him near his mother's face. She looked appalled.

'Just leave him to me.' he said softly.

'What'll you do?'

'I'll make sure he's somewhere to be found.'

Mary said, 'Where?'

'I'll think of somewhere where he can't be missed, and he'll be taken in by someone. A nice family, or,' and he stopped to find the right words. 'There're places, you know... places for the likes of him.' And he left the barn with the towelled baby inside his jacket.

Mary didn't wake until well after midnight, and when she did, she found an Infant Jesus, lying next to her in the straw, with his arms outstretched, palms upwards. Wide intelligent eyes, glowing cheeks and a benign smile upon his little pink lips. How healthy he looked. She carried him home, pressing the plaster-cast baby to her chest.

Her father and mother were blazing when she turned up. They'd been home a short while after taking a Christmas drink with neighbours, thinking that she too was with the youngsters, old enough to partake in the festivities after Midnight Mass.

'I was walking and talking with some friends from school...'

'Walking and talking!' her father spat out. 'Up to no good, I'll be bound. I don't know what's got into you lately my girl, but I'll thrash it out of you one way or another, so I will...'

Her mother said, 'Easy for God's sake, Joe. She's a good girl as you well know. Good as gold.'

'But she's heading the wrong way. I have a hunch she is.'

Vince was in bed by the time his parents returned from Mass. They too, had been socialising with neighbours.

'Where were you, Vince?' his mother whispered as she looked in on him. 'Father Saul was asking for you.'

'Sorry, Mammy. I came over real queer, I was sick on the roadside. Made me late so I slipped in at the back.'

'Oh, it must be something doing the rounds; Mary's daddy said the same. She's been peaky for a week or so. 'Twasn't the same without you on the altar, though. First time you've ever missed serving at Midnight Mass.

'Yeah. I know...'

'Ah, can't be helped, son. You need anything?'

'I'm fine. I think.'

'Good night, God bless, then. See you in the morning.'

It was a night Vince McSweet went over and over in his mind for many years. Especially after he married Magda Steel and they started their family. Three boys: Teddy, Tommy and Liam. And when Liam's own boy was born twenty-two years later on a Christmas Eve, they named him after his grandfather, and called him Vinny.

Vince McSweet wondered if Our Lord and Our Lady were trying to tell him that the Christmas Eve of 1955 was not forgotten.

Mary McAllister never recovered from the trauma and went from an ordinary, well-adjusted schoolgirl to a withdrawn,

165

mentally unstable child, prone to bouts of depression alternating with the wild behaviour of a no-good girl, first tantalising the boys, then shouting and hitting out and calling them the worst kind of fellas, and saying things that made no sense to anyone but her. And her friend, Vince McSweet.

To his shame, Vince broke off the friendship. He couldn't look Mary in the eye. Just couldn't. If truth were known, he wanted shut of that night. Shut of it.

Of course, there was only one place for Mary McAllister. The Laundries. The Magdalen Laundries.

'She'll be out of the way there and be doing something useful,' her father said.

Her mother looked sad and wished she could get to the bottom of it all.

Mary's brother, Declan McAllister said very little – after all, it was nothing to do with him.

Packing up her things in a small portmanteau, the Infant Jesus lay among her meagre clothes as if in a crib.

Mary Mc Allister didn't last long as a 'Maggie', as the laundry women, were called, and was sent to a place for hysterical women. Women who made trouble and told lies about what was going on in the wicked world outside.

At fifty-five, she was sent to the old lunatic asylum near Sligo where she was pumped with experimental drugs for fourteen years, in the hope of improvement. All that did was to rob her of any feistiness she had left in her. Subdued into zombie-like behaviour, she was sent to St Jude's where she remains.

What was left of her brain knew one thing – she recognised the name and the look of that new helper as someone who she knew all those years ago. But she struggled to remember when, or how. Ever since he came to St Jude's she tried to talk to him. Ask him. But the new home-helper hadn't a clue as to what she was saying.

December 24th 2020 10:30pm

Vinny McSweet spent his thirty-fourth birthday caring for the residents of St Jude's, in Knock. He smiled indulgently at the foul-mouthed, Micky Lane, as he placed presents on the side of each bed. Mary McAllister's sixty-four-year-old baby was tight in her arms. 'Happy birthday, Vince,' whispered Vinny, and chuckled.

The 'Marion Shrine of Our Lady' for which Knock is known worldwide, has grown into a significant place of sanctity and worship. Visited by Pope John Paul II in 1979, and by thousands of pilgrims annually, its holy water is credited for countless miracles and unmeasurable mysteries over its 140 years.

The enigma in 1955 of 'St Concepta's Baby' as it became known, was never solved despite the hue and cry; the outrage.

No-one connects the mystery of St Concepta's Baby with the then fifteen-year-olds, Vince McSweet and Mary McAllister – or sixty-five years later, with Vince McSweet's grandson, home-helper, Vinny, and eighty-year Mary McAllister of St Jude's. No-one connects the missing Infant Jesus from the crib at the little church, and the obviously premature dead baby that was left in its place.

The Undead Life of Winnie Eventide

Depending on the light, Winnie Eventide's face appeared to be that of a ten-year-old child, strangely transparent and showing the blue-dark shadows of her bones and veins. In another light, she looked age-old.

This was the eve of Christmas, 1962. Her fawn-coloured hair, usually tousled and sitting like a bird's nest atop her head, didn't look at all out of place as she mingled with fancy-dressed village children: scarecrows, cowboys, rouge-cheeked-dolls, and gossamer fairies. Dressed in the traditional costume of days gone by, her hair was now fastened tight under a Welsh bonnet, topped with a tall black hat. Winnie wore a red-woollen shawl, which she hugged around her body.

I wanted a doll for Christmas, a real, doll-baby that was warm, would move its fingers, and cry: one which I could nurse and be close to. But I didn't get one, simply because there is no such thing as a real doll-baby. I wanted one badly, so it was up to me as to how I managed it.

On a mild Spring Saturday in 1922, I decided I wanted not one, but three doll-babies.

I stole the babies from grandmother's sales basket of wooden and bone things: spoons, bowls, clothes-pegs, combs, rug-hooks, and prodders. I named the babies; Peggy-peg for the one with the broken leg, Dotty-peg for the one with the spotty patterned frock, and Pretty-peg, because she was pretty. I had drawn their faces carefully with a thorn and coloured their cheeks with specks of blood from my pricked finger.

I'd thought my grandmother wouldn't miss a few of the wooden pegs but I was wrong, and she gave me three lashes

168

of a birch twig across my bare legs, saying with each stroke that I was A. Bad. Girl.

I think I was almost ten-years-old – it's difficult to remember so very far back. Especially because I spent a lot of time after in a kind of sleep, which didn't always feel like sleep, but like a living dream. I've never been sure of the difference. Anyway, after grandmother's lashes, I ran off in a sulk.

'And I shan't come back. *Ever*.'

'You'll be back when your stomach says so, Winnie Eventide! We're having that nice rabbit stew, and…'

I didn't hear the rest of her ranting and ran like a brisk wind until I could hardly breathe, away from the tumble-down place we called home in the middle of the woods. My hurt was so great that I cursed her and all my family, and I hoped that I would never see any of them again. That they would die.

Dashing on and on without laying down tracks, I soon became tired and slept awhile on some dried ferns. When I awoke, I had no idea which way to go back.

I asked Peggy-peg, 'What shall I do?'

'Go home,' she answered with a wise look upon her little wooden face.

But no! I went on walking and walking and talking to my babies until I was so far away, I didn't recognise anywhere. I knew I should have turned and gone back the relatively safe way, because I didn't want to meet any of the local Woollen Mill boys on their break. Poor as they were, our brood was far below them and they teased and treated us poorly if they saw us outside our patch, and I was well outside our patch.

I was relieved, though, when I saw the young son of the mill owner, who would surely have more manners.

'Hello, pretty Miss,' he said. 'Would you and your babies like a cup of fresh milk and a biscuit?'

'Of course,' I said, 'yes, we would.' I had never been spoken to before by such a nice young gent.

'Follow me,' he said. I saw him looking all over my dress. I knew it was stained and grubby, but he seemed to like what he saw, and smiled when he added, 'Let's see what we can find.'

I walked slowly alongside him, my legs too tired to move quicker.

'Have you strayed far?'

Too far, I thought, and nodded.

'Nearly there. Just down the path and over that style. There!' He pointed to the rooftops of the woollen mill. I let him help me over the style as if I were quite used to this kind of treatment, and when he put his fingers to his mouth and said '*ssshhhh.*' I copied him and felt as if we were sharing a secret. We crept over a wobbly wooden bridgeway and through one of the dark doors.

'I have my own den, here,' he whispered as we went through a door marked *Old Storeroom*. But it was just a cramped little space at the far end of the stock room, with an easy-chair and an upturned tea-chest with books on top.

He bowed low and said teasingly, 'I'll ring for the maid to get us some tea.'

We both laughed, although I didn't quite understand why.

'But first.' He had stopped smiling. 'We can look at these books.'

Oh, no! I could hardly read. What will he think? And as if he could read my mind, he said, 'They're picture books.'

And so they were. But not like the colourful board-book I had at home which told a story. These pictures were of naked people. And I'm not sure what they were doing. A cold feeling fell over me, and as puzzled as I was, I knew I had been tricked. We were not going to get a cup of milk and biscuits after all.

I threw down the book of rude pictures and wondered why he was showing them to me. *Why?*

Even at my age, I began to understand that this nice young gent was now changed. His face had a strange faraway look to it, and I was frightened.

'Here,' he said, unbuckling his pants. 'We could be like the people in the books, couldn't we?' Then he reached for my skirts, and I tripped over the chair as I tried to pull away. I wailed and screeched to be let out of this place, and I couldn't stop. Couldn't stop no matter how hard he shook me. In the end, he put his hand over my mouth and pressed hard on my throat to stop the noise.

He pressed and pressed, and I couldn't breathe. The last thing I heard was a voice shouting his name: '*Bevan! Where the hell are you? There's work to be done!*'

There was nothing for it but to hide the child behind the bales of cotton and hessian. Bevan Lewis threw her onto a thick layer of sackcloth and as the dust rose, he tossed more remnants of cloth onto her. Then he climbed down the iron ladder and into the Mill itself. First to the floor which held the huge washing and dying tanks, then up to the drying room, the cutting room, and then to the room which housed the weaving looms. The noise was cacophonous.

'I'm here,' he shouted to his father.

Above the noise, he read his father's lips: 'Y'lazy bugger, you've been skiving again – idle hands make work for the devil, so they do. The sooner you're back at school the better...'

When Winnie Eventide went missing, her mother and grandmother, aunts and cousins, poked into every cranny and nook in the woodland, searched in every sheep pen and behind every privy at the bottom of every yard in the village. She was presumed dead, but a local constable dismissed her disappearance saying, 'She's probably run away with the travellers' children, and she'll just turn up one day, like a bad penny.'

Slowly, Winnie opened her eyes. Where was she?

Breathing shallowly, she recognized the pleasant scents: eucalyptus, wormwood, basil and lavender, used to repel insects and moths from the rolls of cloth on which she lay.

She couldn't move. She lay face down, her legs heavily pinned; her arms, one underneath her body and the other bent at the elbow with her hand touching her head. Nothing physical strapped her down except for the certainty that something bad had happened. Her limbs refused to do as she bid them and so she simply lay there and tried to remember what caused the bad feeling in her stomach and the place from where she piddled. Slowly she regained her senses but did not understand them, so it was easier to just lie still, to lie perfectly still and stay her mind; to try to breathe without her throat hurting. She felt for her peg-dolls, safe in her pocket.

There she stayed, as night finally stole the day.

And she slept.

Shivering, she awoke as something scuttled over her arm, and something else shifted in the rafters. She swallowed, desperately needing a drink but her throat closed painfully, and she felt her tears, hot and salty as they seeped between her dry lips. Her skin itched all over and she was conscious of the harsh sacking against her cheek.

Winnie thought she heard her name being called, but she was unable to respond. It was safer to stay where she was, clinging tight to Peggy-peg, who knew what it was

172

like to be broken. She escaped into sleep again, her peg-doll babies her only comfort. She wanted to be in the place she was before the bad thing happened.

Just before first light, as she sank deeper into the folds of her sack shroud, little Winnie Eventide departed the life she knew.

But she was neither dead nor alive.

No-one knew where she was that Sunday morning when the bell of St Celenyn beckoned the faithful to the service at eight, nor when the chapel door opened at eleven. In Sunday School at 2:30, the children prayed to Jesus that she would return in time for tea, because it was Sunday, and in their world, there would be custard and jelly and maybe stories before bed.

Pretending he knew nothing of the missing girl, Bevan Lewis laid low until he left the village to return to his school.

What I missed most was the fresh air and open skies. Here, in the half-day-half-night, the only things I had to play with were my peggy-babies and the dust motes, which danced in the meagre sunlight peeping in from the cobwebby windows. Time dragged, and I spent most of it in and out of sleep. It might be weeks before anyone came up to the store-room to find some long-forgotten item or to dump more broken things one on top of the other.

During the first decade, time saw to it that Peggy-peg, Dotty-peg and Pretty-peg succumbed to mice and moths. They became small piles of sawdust and scraps of cotton. So once again, I had no-one at all to nurse and be close to. I was miserable until I met Bessie and Dora, two old mannequins who had also been thrown into a corner, and Dumpty: a patchy, three-legged dressmaker's dummy.

173

From their old stock-room, they'd been exploring a corridor which led them to this room, and found me!

Our days were spent to the sound of the clackety-clacking machines, from which spilled yards and yards of colourful Welsh tapestry, which we watched from our hidden vantage point. At night, the three bickered as to who should show me around the mill.

They, by the nature of their past closeness to humans, and I, by my new-found existence, found solace as something between living and dead: together, we became the undead.

Their knowledge was foreign to me, and mine to them, but between us, we shared a lot and learned a lot, and we got by very well. I taught the three dummies to dance, in little jerky steps that even Dumpty could manage, and they taught me to stand in a petrified state: inflexible, because we often had to rush into a rigid position if one of the hands came up to our room.

Playing, we dressed up in out-of-season skirts and dresses, and the moth-eaten costumes we found in trunks and boxes. Bessie loved to wear a faded red cape with white fur around the hood – a left-over from one of the Mill's Christmas displays. Dora could never make up her mind, while Dumpty wore whatever was nearest, and I liked one of the children's Welsh costumes used to celebrate St David's Day on the 1st March.

Talking, we shared our stories. Despite none of my new friends having been into the outside world, they were familiar with many things, because they had listened for years to the girls and women during their work-breaks; they heard secrets and gossip. They remembered the time all those years ago when I had disappeared, and how everybody thought I'd run away with the travellers' children.

174

But I put them right.

They didn't like my story about the mill owner's son.

Afterwards, Bessie said, 'One day, you may have an opportunity to get even with him.'

I told her that I couldn't think of anything that would make me feel even with him, and Dora said she'd heard that 'revenge is best served cold', and that I should think about that, but I didn't understand and started to cry to think that Bevan Lewis would never be punished for the bad thing he did to me.

That set off Dumpty who became cross, and he said we should stop thinking ill-thoughts but to think about nice things, and he reminded us that it would soon be Christmas; therefore we should look forward to eavesdropping on the young girl-hands to hear of what they were hoping to get in their stockings, and on the women who spoke about all the things they were making for their families, and how thrilled they were to be having two extra days off work. I must admit their gleefulness cheered me up a little, and I realised how lucky I was to have found my three friends, and how lonely I should have been had I not.

So, in trying to push Bevan Lewis far from our minds, we concentrated on things that made us smile, including making presents for each other. Here, we were lucky because over the years, tossed aside and unwanted stock came our way by the box-full: skeins of wool, glue, rags, yards of spoiled cloth, rusted tools. Having everything at our disposal, we used them all, spending hours huddled in the light of the mucky windows. I carved wooden puzzles for Bessie, wove a scarf for Dora, and helped Dumpty to fashion three shoes out of old leather scraps! My favourite present was from Dora – a red shawl made from patches of soft, Welsh wool, which was roomy enough to wrap right around me.

More than once, that shawl gave me great comfort. One such time was when I was alone, and Bevan Lewis, now a man with a wife and son, ventured into the store-room. I was pleased to see he looked unnerved, as if the spirit of his wickedness was watching. But it was me who had an evil eye upon him. My body automatically recoiled from his very presence, yet I managed to keep statue-still as I watched from between the rolls of cloth.

His presence left me shaky and withdrawn for a while, and my three friends tried to comfort me – Dora wrapped me up warm in the roomy, red shawl.

On many occasions, Bevan Lewis came within a few yards of me. Of course he didn't recognise me at all. I had obviously been obliterated from his mind – I was just a replica of a small human being which may have been used to model children's coats and hats and capes in the famous Welsh tapestry. But I never forgot his face, nor his eyes, nor his voice – not in all these years. He still haunted me when I was asleep or awake and in my in-between state. I saw his features in his own son and in his grandchild, a new-born little girl, called Clara, whom we watched him show off to everyone as if she were his – his real baby doll.

Hidden away, Winnie, the child who never grew out of childhood, was now nearly fifty-years-old, but still had a hankering for the doll-baby she didn't get for Christmas all those years ago.

One early evening, after the Mill was closed, I wandered down to the shop floor, searching for anything I could find for us to play with. I heard two people talking, and I went still as a statue, before I realised it was Bevan Lewis' son and wife, selecting a bolt of cloth. There, just out of their sight, I saw the pram. Quietly, I sidled alongside it, and there she was – sleeping baby Clara!

She was so like her grandfather. She opened her new-baby-eyes and looked at me for the longest time. I couldn't take my eyes away from hers, until she slowly closed them again, as if to say *'...I know, I know...'* I could not resist touching the cheek of this infant whose grandfather had robbed me of my outside life, had committed me to forty years of dusty, dirty, moth-eaten fabric; to crevices, cubby-holes, and dark corners, with no real doll-baby. With no chance of ever having a real baby at all.

Old Mr Lewis had long-since died, and as the decades went by, the old stockroom became choc-a-block with junk and about to fall in on itself.

Often, we heard mention of a clear-out.

'This lot'll have to go... and the sooner the better...' It was Bevan Lewis directing his mill-hands. Hearing his voice, I shuddered as I remembered his offer to me – fresh milk and biscuits for my babies. After four long decades, even his voice could make me shudder. He continued, 'For God's sake let's get rid of it all once and for all.'

I was very frightened, but anger overtook my fear and almost choked me as he kicked out at us, going on, 'Especially these damn, dumb dummies – they give me the creeps.' He looked long and hard at us, his face twisting in distaste and his voice spiteful.

After a moment of thought, he smirked. 'We'll give the village kids a treat. A party like no other... Yes, a bonfire, early on Christmas Eve. Toffee apples and baked potatoes – and a fancy-dress parade!'

So, he was to burn me, was he? On the Christmas Eve of 1962.

The locals helped to clear out all the wooden crates and boxes, the rotten timbers, the rat-chewed bolts of cloth. And us, the dummies.

177

Dressed in our make-believe clothes of woven tapestry, Bessie was wearing her matching skirt and jacket. She looked so pretty that one young man danced around with her, almost tripping over her ram-rod stiff body. Dora wore a long woollen cape, and Dumpty was in a mismatch of incongruous clothes topped with a beret set at a jaunty angle. I wore my favourite traditional Welsh costume, and wrapped around my shoulders, I draped my red woollen shawl.

We wept as we said goodbye. Dora, Bessie, Dumpty and me. Our tears mingled as we clumsily clung together. The men threw us into a cart, and trundled us down to the playing field to feed the fire.

This was the first time in forty years I'd set foot outside the mill, so I crawled out of the cart to look around at the open space that I should have grown up in, maybe married and had real babies. My legs wouldn't work properly, but no-one paid me any attention as I hobbled along, into the crowd.

The whole village turned out. Bevan Lewis strutted around with his wife and son, and the new granddaughter in her pram. Shouting orders to everyone, he told the mothers to stand back and to keep their children away from the flames. But this was a party like no other, with the most spectacular bonfire the village had ever seen, and the children danced around and around in their fancy-dress clothes, excitedly singing and chanting.

Eventually, I managed to stand near Bevan Lewis' son and daughter-in-law and baby Clara, who was half-hidden beneath layers of pram covers. To them, I was just another dressed-up child.

Their faces shone with a red glow as the young family

enjoyed the heat from the bonfire. As they celebrated with the rest of the village, I took the opportunity to snatch up the tiny infant. I felt the movements of her little body against my breast. It would be my last chance to hold a real baby close. Just for a second, I told myself. Just for one second.

But like everything, it didn't last.

To my horror, I watched the Mill cart pull up beside the bonfire, and I saw my friends staring out at the crowd. I thought they were looking for me, and I wanted to be with them. A sadness I didn't know I could experience filled my heart as I stumbled towards them, legs stiff and inanimate, and fell against the cart. I was abruptly hauled up and tossed on top of Bessie, Dora and Dumpty. Reunited, the four of us were doused in paraffin, and one by one, the village men flung us onto the fire.

As the flames rose around us, I, Winnie Eventide, held tight to baby Clara in my comforting, red woollen shawl.

First published in an anthology *Dark Reflections* by Annwn Press (Imprint of Bangor University) 2023

About the Author

After gaining a First Class Hons at Bangor University: MArts in 'English Literature with Creative Writing' 2015-2019, she completed a Masters at the University of Chester: 'Writing and Publishing Fiction' 2019-2020. Her common-folk biography, *My Whole World, Penmaenmawr* was published by Old Bakehouse Publications, Abertillery, in 2000. *Lilies of the Valley*, a Gothic, family saga, made the strong longlist in the Cinnamon Press Debut Novel Award 2018, and retitled *The Stain,* the longlist in the Indie Novella. Her unpublished picaresque novel, *Quinn*, made the Cinnamon Press 'Mention with Honours' in 2020.

In partnership with co-writer, Judy Price, her collection of 'uncanny', short stories, *Cautiously Tiptoeing... Out of the Light*, was published in October 2020, and *Cautiously Tiptoeing... Into the Thirteen Days of Christmas*, in December.

A series of six children's stories, is set in the National Trust's Bodnant Garden 'to educate and entertain children'. Her first children's book, beautifully illustrated by Laura Stenhouse, *Timothy Crumble Explores Bodnant Garden* was published in April 2021.

The above publications are available from Amazon.

Acknowledgements

Thank you to Gill James and the dedicated team at Bridge House Publishing for the opportunity to present my first solo collection of short stories, *There's More to Life than Death*. So much goes on behind the scenes in a publishing house to present the best finished article from its tentative beginnings, to its place on the bookshelves.

I'm indebted to my fellow-painter friend, Terry Mart, for the book cover. He captured the image of a particular derelict house in woodland, just as I imagined it. Between Terry, and Bridge House designer Martin James, they portrayed the atmosphere of the title story.

The art of writing a publishable book is a long process; I do not forget my fellow writers who encourage and cheer each other on. Thank you all.

Like to Read More Work Like This?

Then sign up to our mailing list and download our free collection of short stories, *Magnetism*. Sign up now to receive this free e-book and also to find out about all of our new publications and offers.

Sign up here:
   http://eepurl.com/gbpdVz

Please Leave a Review

Reviews are so important to writers. Please take the time to review this book. A couple of lines is fine.

Reviews help the book to become more visible to buyers. Retailers will promote books with multiple reviews.

This in turn helps us to sell more books... And then we can afford to publish more books like this one.

Leaving a review is very easy.

Go to https://amzn.to/3XoPLJA, scroll down the left-hand side of the Amazon page and click on the 'Write a customer review' button.

Other writing by Anne Forrest

Timothy Crumble Explores Bodnant Garden
Independently published

The six stories can be seen as stepping-stones. The first one is an
introduction to Timothy Crumble and to the garden, with each
subsequent story progressing to be of interest to older children (up
to the age of about 99...) where I introduce some magical creatures
and their habitats. Timothy and Benji Crumble, their cousins,
William, George, Anna and Ishbel Harker are fictitious, and so are
their adventures, but they take place in a real setting in North Wales
- and as much as these children would like to explore on their own,
they must take an adult with them!

'A well written tale with beautiful, colourful illustrations. A joy to
read to your children.' (*Amazon*)

Order from Amazon:

Paperback: ISBN 979-8-738429-33-0

Cautiously Tiptoeing… Out of the Light
Independently published

In the uncanny world of *Cautiously Tiptoeing…Out of the Light*, one can experience something beyond everyday happenings; beyond and behind the comfortable. Life itself is often just a footstep away from balance; from the status quo. Whether one steps gingerly and stealthily or with confident exploration, often the fantastical occurs when least expected.

Venturing out of the light the reader can stroll between rural Wales or Spain, walk in the Texas panhandle, wander along the Atchafalaya River, climb the Miners' Path on Mount Snowdon; visit a London cemetery, a Victorian asylum, and an apothecary shop. They can meander back a couple of centuries, and then stalk the 1960s. Noticing intertextuality, and recognising a familiar fairy tale, they may abandon themselves to the possibility of anthropomorphism, and other worlds altogether.

'I found these stories captivating, the quality of the writing was extremely high and I can't wait for the authors next publication.' (*Amazon*)

Order from Amazon:

Paperback: ISBN 979-8-694909-34-1
eBook: ASIN: B08HX5N4LD

Cautiously Tiptoeing… Into the Thirteen Days of Christmas
Independently published

In the uncanny world of *Cautiously Tiptoeing...into the Thirteen Days of Christmas* one can experience a stocking full of flash fiction, short stories and poetry. Forrest and Price hope their Christmas offering will bring unexpected gifts. All will be revealed when you unwrap the pretty Christmas paper to expose the contents. Reaching in to the tip of the stocking toe, your fingers may touch a familiar shape, only to find that it contains something else altogether. Venturing in to the many aspects of this season, the reader can experience various takes on the traditional and ancient story, learn a little about Santa Claus' anthropomorphic other, Krampus, inveigle their way in to characters' secret wishes and sample an alternative to well-known Carols and Christmas stories. There are many meanings of the word 'uncanny'. Let us settle for 'disquieting'.

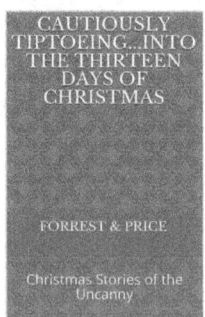

'The stories are fascinating and all have a unusual or uncanny twist to them. It makes compulsive reading.' (*Amazon*)

Order from Amazon:

Paperback: ISBN 979-8-578369-23-0
eBook: ASIN: B08QG3SWGC

Other Publications by Bridge House

The Story Weaver
by Sally Zigmond

Story-telling has often been associated with weaving and
spinning. All is craft, cleverness and magic.

Here indeed we have a colourful mix of beautifully crafted
stories. Some are sad and others bring us hope. There are
tensions in relationships, fear of the unknown coupled with
surprising empathy, and accidents of birth. Death wishes are
reversed, sometimes but not always, and so are lives in other
realties. People's stories intersect as they wait for a bus. An old
cello causes havoc. A church clock always strikes twice… or
does it? Match-making goes wrong until it goes right. And so
much more.

"A wonderful collection of interesting tales. A real mixture
that will delight all readers." *(Amazon)*

Order from Amazon:

Paperback: ISBN 978-1-914199-54-7
eBook: ISBN 978-1-914199-55-4

The Adventures of Iris and Zach
by I.L. Green

Iris and Zach have an uneasy but intriguing run.

A vast patchwork landscape of life is displayed through stories relating both the wonder and absurdity we all recognize. With a focus on mental health, these stories take the reader from incarceration to freedom, fear to comfort. There are celebrations of life and poetic lows. The Yin and Yang aspects of life are recognized in new and deliberate examples that instil thoughtfulness and occasionally a smile.

Order from Amazon:

Paperback: ISBN 978-1-914199-34-9
eBook: ISBN 978-1-914199-35-6

A Gentle Nudge
by Mason Bushell

Stories to soothe your soul.

In a world drowning in negativity and dark events, we all need a little light and hope. With a little adventure, romance and even music, these short stories will give your hopes and dreams a nudge as they draw a smile.

A Gentle Nudge by Mason Bushell wraps you in calm.

Order from Amazon:

Paperback: ISBN 978-1-914199-42-4
eBook: ISBN 978-1-914199-43-1

www.ingramcontent.com/pod-product-compliance
Lightning Source LLC
Chambersburg PA
CBHW061207170626
46809CB00003B/1272